Index

CHAPTER 1: INTRODUCTION TO CYBERSECURITY
- What is cybersecurity and why is it important to protect computer systems?   5
- Overview of the main cyber threats   7
- The three fundamental components of cybersecurity: prevention, detection and response   16
- Basic principles for the protection of information systems   20

CHAPTER 2: FUNDAMENTALS OF CRYPTOGRAPHY
- Key concepts of cryptography   21
- Symmetric encryption algorithms   22
- Asymmetric encryption algorithms   24
- Public key cryptography and private key cryptography   26
- Correct use of encryption to protect sensitive data   28

CHAPTER 3: NETWORK SECURITY
- Basic concepts of networks and communication protocols   31
- Common threats and attacks on networks   33
- Tools and techniques for protecting networks   36
- Firewall, IDS (Intrusion Detection System) and IPS (Intrusion Prevention System)   40

CHAPTER 4: APPLICATION SECURITY
- Main vulnerabilities in software applications   46
- Testing applications to identify security flaws   49
- Best practices for developing secure applications   52
- Patch and update management   55

CHAPTER 5: DATA PROTECTION
- Basic principles of data protection　　　　　　　　58
- Data encryption techniques　　　　　　　　　　　62
- Backing up and restoring data　　　　　　　　　　64
- Management of access to sensitive data　　　　　70

CHAPTER 6: THREAT AND SECURITY INCIDENT MANAGEMENT
- Monitoring and detection of cyber threats　　　　74
- Security Incident Response　　　　　　　　　　　78
- Business continuity planning and post-incident recovery　　81
- Role of policies and procedures in safety management　　84

CHAPTER 7: PHYSICAL AND ENVIRONMENTAL SAFETY
- Security of premises and data centers　　　　　　87
- Physical access control　　　　　　　　　　　　91
- Protection of devices and physical storage media　　94
- Waste management and secure data disposal　　96

CHAPTER 8: PRIVACY AND REGULATORY COMPLIANCE
- Fundamental principles of privacy and protection of personal data 99
- Legislation and regulations on privacy　　　　　103
- Best practices for managing personal data　　　106
- Compliance with industry regulations and standards　　111

CHAPTER 9: MOBILE SECURITY AND BYOD
- Mobile and app security　　　　　　　　　　　115
- BYOD policies and best practices for the safe use of personal devices in the workplace　　119
- Managing risks associated with the use of mobile devices　　122

CHAPTER 10: CYBERSECURITY LAWS
- Cybersecurity legislation in USA   125
- Cybersecurity legislation in Europe   127
- Cybersecurity laws in the rest of the world   129

CHAPTER 11: EMERGING TRENDS IN CYBERSECURITY
- Artificial intelligence and machine learning in cybersecurity   131
- Security of the IoT (Internet of Things) and smart cities   133
- Emerging threats and future challenges for cybersecurity   135
- Role of skills and training in the field of cybersecurity   137

Intro

The book "Principles and Practices of Cybersecurity: Foundations and Applications" provides a comprehensive overview of the theory and applications of cybersecurity. It addresses emerging threats and challenges in cybersecurity and presents fundamental principles, defense strategies, and best practices for protecting sensitive systems, networks, and data. The aim of the book is to provide a solid foundation of theoretical and practical knowledge for students, professionals and enthusiasts in the sector.

Introduction to cybersecurity

What is cybersecurity and why it is important to protect computer systems

Cybersecurity is a rapidly growing field that deals with protecting computer systems from cyber threats and attacks. In an age where digital technology permeates every aspect of our lives, cybersecurity has become a key priority. In this introductory section, we will explore what exactly the term "cybersecurity" means and why it is crucial to protect computer systems. Cybersecurity focuses on defending computer systems, networks, applications and data from unauthorized access, damage, theft or destruction. Cyberattacks can come from malicious hackers, cybercriminals, rival organizations, or even internal employees. These threats can have devastating consequences, including financial damage, loss of reputation, invasion of privacy, and even disruption of critical services. To effectively protect computer systems, it is critical to understand the key cyber threats we face. In this section, we will provide an overview of the most common threats that organizations and individuals face in the context of cybersecurity. One of the most prevalent threats is phishing attacks, in which attackers try to obtain personal or financial information via deceptive emails, text messages, or phone calls. Other threats include malware, ransomware, brute force attacks, distributed denial of service (DDoS), vulnerability exploits, and social engineering. To create a robust cybersecurity system, you need to take a comprehensive approach that includes three key components: prevention, detection, and response. In this section, we will look in detail at each of these components and their role in protecting computer systems. Prevention is a crucial aspect of cybersecurity and focuses on putting preventative measures in place to minimize the risk of attacks. These measures include implementing firewalls, using antivirus and antispyware software, encrypting sensitive data, and enforcing strict security policies. Detection of cyber threats is just as important as prevention. Attacks can escape prevention mechanisms, so it is essential to have intrusion detection and network activity monitoring systems in place to spot signs of possible attacks. The use of logging systems and data analytics can help identify suspicious or anomalous activity that could indicate an attack in progress. Responding to cyber attacks is a critical element of cybersecurity. When an attack is detected, you must respond promptly to mitigate damage and restore security. This may include disconnecting the affected system from the network, identifying and isolating the malware, communicating with the relevant authorities, and remediating the vulnerabilities that enabled the attack. To protect computer systems effectively, it is essential to follow some basic principles. In this section, we will explore some of these fundamental principles for ensuring the security of computer systems. One of the key principles is to apply a defense in depth approach. This means using a combination of multiple security measures, such as firewalls, antivirus, multi-factor authentication, data encryption and cybersecurity training to ensure vulnerabilities are addressed from multiple angles. Another important principle is constant vigilance and risk management. Technology and cyber threats continue to evolve, so you need to stay informed about new trends and take the necessary steps to mitigate risks. Risk assessment, business continuity planning and implementation of robust security policies are an integral part of this process.

Overview of the main cyber threats

In our increasingly interconnected society, cyber threats have become increasingly pervasive and sophisticated. In this section, we will explore the main cyber threats that organizations and individuals face in the context of cybersecurity. We will dedicate a page to each type of attack to examine them in depth.

Phishing attacks

Cybersecurity is a discipline that deals with protecting computer systems from malicious threats and attacks. In the context of cybersecurity theory, one of the key aspects to understand is the concept of phishing and its security implications. Phishing represents one of the main threats in the cybersecurity landscape. Attackers use phishing as a way to obtain sensitive personal or financial information by deceiving victims. Phishing attacks typically occur via fraudulent emails, text messages, or phone calls. To fully understand phishing, it is important to examine the tactics used by attackers. They try to create convincing messages that appear to come from trustworthy entities, such as banks or online services. This way, they try to make the message seem authentic and convince victims to share their information. They use visual elements such as logos, colors and writing styles similar to those of official communications to deceive people into trusting the message. Another crucial aspect of phishing is the use of human emotions. Attackers use fear, urgency, or curiosity to push victims into immediate, reckless actions. For example, they may send an email stating that your account has been compromised and that you need to take immediate action to avoid negative consequences. This tactic puts pressure on people, pushing them to react without carefully evaluating the authenticity of the message. To protect yourself from phishing, it is essential to adopt conscious security practices. First of all, it is important to carefully evaluate the messages you receive. Taking the time to analyze the appearance and content of the message can help identify any signs of phishing, such as spelling mistakes or unusual requests for personal or financial information. Additionally, it is essential to avoid clicking on suspicious or untrustworthy links in phishing messages. If the link seems suspicious or you are unsure of its legitimacy, it is best not to open it. You can manually type the website URL into your browser or use a reliable search engine to access the site in question. Keeping your software updated is another important practice to protect yourself from phishing threats. Newer versions of operating systems, programs, and applications often include security patches that help prevent vulnerabilities from being exploited by cyberattacks. Finally, using two-factor authentication (2FA) can provide an additional layer of security. Enabling 2FA requires a second verification method, in addition to a password, to access an account. This can make it more difficult for attackers to compromise your account even if they manage to obtain your password. In conclusion, phishing represents one of the most widespread and deceptive threats in cybersecurity. Understanding the tactics used by attackers and adopting informed security practices are key to protecting yourself from such attacks. Carefully evaluating messages, avoiding clicking on suspicious links, keeping your software up to date, and using two-factor authentication are just some of the measures that can contribute to better cybersecurity against phishing.

Malware

Speaking of cybersecurity, a crucial aspect to understand is malware. Malware is malicious software created with the intent to compromise the security of computer systems. These malicious software can take many forms, such as viruses, worms, Trojans, ransomware, and spyware. Let's start with viruses, which are among the most common malware. Viruses are designed to infect executable files or other system files. Once executed, the virus can replicate and spread within the system, damaging or destroying files present. This can cause a variety of problems, such as loss of critical data or system malfunction. Another form of malware is worms. Unlike viruses, worms are capable of propagating themselves without user intervention. By exploiting security vulnerabilities in systems or networks, worms quickly spread from computer to computer. They can cause network congestion and degrade the performance of affected systems. Trojans, on the other hand, are malware that present themselves as legitimate or harmless software, but which actually hide malicious functionality. Users can be tricked into installing a Trojan by opening suspicious email attachments or downloading software from untrusted sources. Once installed, the Trojan can allow an attacker to gain remote access to the system, steal sensitive data, or damage the system itself. Another worrying form of malware is ransomware. Ransomware is designed to encrypt data on the infected system, making it inaccessible to the user. Attackers then demand payment, usually in cryptocurrencies, to provide the decryption key and restore access to the data. This type of attack can cause serious financial and operational damage to affected organizations and individuals. Finally, spyware is malware that secretly monitors and collects users' personal information, such as browsing activities, login credentials, or financial information. This data can be used for fraudulent purposes or sold to third parties. Spyware is often installed without the user's consent, for example by downloading free software or opening suspicious links. It is essential to understand the different types of malware and the risks associated with them in order to take appropriate security measures. This includes installing up-to-date antivirus and antispyware software, regularly updating your operating system and applications, downloading software only from trusted sources, and educating users about safe browsing and file handling practices. Fighting malware is a key aspect of cybersecurity and requires a combination of technological tools, good security practices and user awareness.

Ransomware

Let's now talk about ransomware, a particularly insidious form of malware that represents a significant threat in the field of cybersecurity. Ransomware is designed to encrypt data on infected systems, making it inaccessible to the legitimate user. Attackers behind ransomware demand payment, usually in cryptocurrencies, in exchange for the decryption key needed to restore access to the data. Ransomware commonly spreads through phishing emails, compromised websites, or exploits of vulnerabilities in systems. Once ransomware infects a system, it starts encrypting files, rendering them unusable. This can have devastating consequences for organizations and individuals, as critical and sensitive data is rendered inaccessible and can lead to financial losses and business disruptions. An important aspect to consider regarding ransomware is the need to take preventative measures. User awareness is critical to recognizing and avoiding social engineering tactics used by attackers. Users need to be trained on how to recognize phishing emails, suspicious websites and other types of online scams. Additionally, it is crucial to keep your operating system and applications updated with the latest security patches. Developers constantly release updates to fix known vulnerabilities and improve software security. Applying these patches regularly reduces the risk of compromise by ransomware. Another essential practice for protecting yourself from ransomware is to make regular data backups. Backups allow you to restore your data in the event of a ransomware attack, without having to pay the ransom. It is important to keep backups on separate devices or offline storage solutions to prevent backups from also being encrypted during an attack. Finally, using up-to-date antivirus and antimalware solutions can help detect and block ransomware before it infects your system. These tools are able to identify typical ransomware behaviors and block them before they cause damage. In conclusion, ransomware poses a serious threat to data security. It is critical to take preventative measures, such as user training, software updates, regular data backups, and the use of antivirus solutions, to effectively protect yourself from these attacks.

Brute force attacks

Brute force attacks pose a significant threat to cybersecurity. Attackers use this technique to try to guess a password or cryptographic key by repeating a wide range of possible combinations. These attacks rely on the computing power of modern computers which can perform a large number of attempts in a very short time. The goal of brute force attacks is to bypass authentication mechanisms to gain unauthorized access to a system or account. These attacks can be targeted at various access points, such as user account passwords, encryption keys, or PIN codes. Attackers can target online services, Wi-Fi networks, applications, or any other system that relies on passwords for authentication. To protect yourself from brute force attacks, it is crucial to take appropriate security measures. Below, we will discuss some best practices that can help prevent such attacks. First and foremost, it's crucial to use strong passwords. Passwords should be complex and difficult to guess. We recommend using a combination of uppercase and lowercase letters, numbers, and special characters. Avoid common or easy-to-guess passwords, such as birth dates or family names. Another effective measure is to limit the number of login attempts allowed. Imposing restrictions on attempts to access systems can make brute force attacks less effective. For example, after a certain number of failed attempts, the system may lock your account or impose a delay before allowing further login attempts. An additional recommended security measure is the adoption of two-factor authentication (2FA). With two-factor authentication, in addition to the password, an additional form of verification is required, such as a code generated by an application on the phone or a fingerprint. This provides an additional layer of security, since even if an attacker manages to discover the password, they will not have access without the second factor of authentication. Additionally, it is important to keep your systems and applications updated with the latest security patches. Vulnerabilities in software can be exploited by attackers to carry out brute force attacks. Security patches released by software vendors often contain fixes for these vulnerabilities, so it is essential to install them promptly to reduce the risk of attacks. Finally, it is advisable to carefully monitor access logs and implement intrusion detection systems to promptly identify and respond to brute force attacks. These tools help you spot suspicious or repetitive activity that could be indicative of an ongoing attack. In summary, brute force attacks pose a significant threat to cybersecurity. To protect against such attacks, it is important to use strong passwords, limit login attempts, implement two-factor authentication, keep systems updated, and carefully monitor user activity. These measures help strengthen system security and mitigate risks associated with brute force attacks.

DDoS (Distributed Denial of Service)

DDoS attacks, also known as Distributed Denial of Service, are a form of cyber attack that aims to overload a system, application or network infrastructure with a high volume of traffic, making them inaccessible to legitimate users. These attacks exploit a network of compromised devices, called a botnet, that act in a coordinated manner to send a large amount of requests or data to the target system. The goal is to overwhelm system resources, such as bandwidth, processing capacity, or memory, causing a denial of service to legitimate users. DDoS attacks can take different forms and can be classified based on their characteristics. Some common examples include network-level flood attacks, in which a huge amount of connection requests are sent to overload network resources, and amplification attacks, in which the response of a server or service is exploited to generate a much higher volume of traffic. These attacks can cause severe damage to organizations, including extended downtime, loss of reputation, loss of sensitive data, and significant financial costs. Therefore, it is crucial to implement robust defense measures to protect against DDoS attacks. Solutions to mitigate DDoS attacks include the use of intruder detection and prevention systems (IDS/IPS), advanced firewalls, load balancers, IP filters and DDoS protection services offered by specialized vendors. Additionally, it is important to have a well-defined incident response plan that allows you to promptly address DDoS attacks when they occur. This plan should include early identification of attacks, isolation of affected resources, communication with Internet service providers, and forensic analysis to understand the origin and motivations of the attack. In conclusion, DDoS attacks represent a significant threat to cybersecurity and require adequate protection measures to mitigate their negative effects. Understanding these threats and implementing appropriate defense solutions are critical to maintaining the security and reliability of systems and networks.

The three fundamental components of cybersecurity: prevention, detection and response

Protecting information systems requires taking a comprehensive approach that includes three key components: prevention, detection and response. In this section, we will delve deeper into each of these components and their crucial role in defending computer systems from cyber threats.

Prevention

Prevention is a fundamental step to guarantee the security of IT systems. On this page, we will take an in-depth look at strategies and preventative measures that can be taken to minimize the risk of cyber attacks. We will discuss system hardening practices, which include applying regular security patches, securely configuring network devices, managing user privileges, and implementing robust security policies. We'll also explore the importance of cybersecurity education and user awareness, providing guidance on how to recognize common threats, avoid the pitfalls of phishing attacks, and protect your login credentials.

Detection

Cyber threat detection is essential to identify attacks early and respond promptly. On this page, we will look at the techniques and tools used for intrusion detection and network activity monitoring. We will discuss the importance of system logs and security events, which can provide vital information about anomalous or suspicious activity. We will also explore the use of intrusion detection systems (IDS) and advanced threat detection (ATD) systems to identify signs of an attack in progress. We'll delve into analyzing logs and data streams, using artificial intelligence and machine learning algorithms to identify attack patterns, and implementing automated alerts and notifications to flag potential threats.

Respond

The ability to respond promptly to cyber attacks is critical to mitigating damage and restoring system security. On this page, we will review the steps of responding to cybersecurity incidents. We will discuss the importance of incident response planning, which includes creating a well-trained incident response team, defining roles and responsibilities, and implementing a communications plan. We will explore digital forensics techniques used to identify the source of attacks and gather evidence, as well as how to recover systems and data after an incident. We will also discuss the importance of communicating with the appropriate authorities, such as law enforcement or cybersecurity agencies, to report the incident and cooperate in the investigation.

Basic principles for the protection of computer systems

Protecting information systems requires the application of basic principles that form the foundation for a solid cybersecurity strategy. On this page, we'll look at some of these core principles in detail. One of the key principles is the application of a defense in depth approach. This means using a combination of multiple security measures to ensure that vulnerabilities are addressed from different angles. We will discuss the importance of implementing firewalls, intrusion detection systems, intrusion prevention systems, spam filters, multi-factor authentication solutions, and data encryption. We will also explore the need to carry out regular security audits, risk assessments and penetration tests to identify any weaknesses and ensure complete protection. Another important principle is constant vigilance and risk management. Technology and cyber threats continue to evolve, so it is essential to stay informed about new trends and take the necessary steps to mitigate risks. We will discuss the importance of keeping systems and software updated with the latest security patches, as well as promoting a cybersecurity culture within your organization. We will also explore the importance of implementing risk management processes, which include identifying and assessing risks, implementing appropriate controls, and planning for business continuity in the event of a security breach.

FUNDAMENTALS OF CRYPTOGRAPHY

Key concepts of cryptography

Cryptography is a fundamental discipline in computer security that deals with protecting the confidentiality and integrity of data. In this section, we will explore the key concepts of encryption and its importance in protecting sensitive information. Cryptography relies on the use of mathematical algorithms to transform data into an incomprehensible form, called ciphertext, which can only be read by those who have the correct key to decrypt it. This encryption process makes the data inaccessible to unwanted third parties, ensuring the confidentiality of the information. Additionally, encryption plays a vital role in ensuring data integrity. Using cryptographic algorithms, it is possible to verify whether data has been modified or altered during transmission or storage. This helps detect any unauthorized manipulation and ensures that the data has been received or stored in its original form. Throughout this section, we will explore different types of encryption, including symmetric and asymmetric encryption. We will discuss the differences between these two cryptographic approaches and the situations in which they are most appropriate. We will also look at the most common cryptographic algorithms used in both forms of encryption, such as AES (Advanced Encryption Standard) for symmetric encryption and RSA (Rivest-Shamir-Adleman) for asymmetric encryption. Cryptography is a complex but essential concept in information security.

Symmetric encryption algorithms

Symmetric encryption is an important cryptographic technique that involves the use of a single key to encrypt and decrypt data. On this page, we will explore the basic principles of symmetric encryption and its most common algorithms. The fundamental principle of symmetric encryption is that the sender and recipient share a secret key, which is used to encrypt and decrypt data. The secret key must remain secret to ensure the security of communications. The most common symmetric encryption algorithms include the Advanced Encryption Standard (AES), the Data Encryption Standard (DES), and the Triple Data Encryption Standard (3DES). AES is one of the most widely used and has demonstrated good resistance to current attack techniques. DES, on the other hand, is an older algorithm, but still used in some legacy applications. The choice of symmetric encryption algorithm depends on several factors, including desired security, processing speed, and system requirements. It is important to carefully consider these factors in order to select the algorithm best suited to your specific needs. During symmetric encryption, data is divided into blocks and each block is encrypted separately using the secret key. It is essential to use a secure key generation method and keep the secret key protected from unauthorized access. Another widely used symmetric encryption algorithm is Blowfish. Blowfish is known for its flexibility in choosing key length, allowing it to use longer keys than other symmetric algorithms. This feature makes it suitable for protecting sensitive data that requires greater security. A key aspect in symmetric cryptography is key security. The secret key must be handled securely to avoid exposure to unauthorized third parties. Key generation mechanisms must be robust and ensure that the keys generated are random and long enough to resist cracking attempts. Furthermore, key management in the context of symmetric cryptography requires the implementation of secure protocols for key distribution and updating. This is especially important in environments where the key needs to be shared between multiple entities. It is also crucial to consider the scalability of symmetric encryption algorithms, especially when dealing with large amounts of data to be encrypted and decrypted. Processing speed and efficiency are critical factors to ensure adequate data protection without compromising system performance. Another notable symmetric encryption algorithm is Twofish. Twofish is a highly secure and robust algorithm that can be used to protect a wide range of data, including files, emails and network communications. Its flexibility and ability to support different key sizes make it a popular option for applications requiring increased security. In addition to the security of the algorithm itself, the correct implementation of the symmetric encryption algorithm is critical to ensuring data protection. Implementation errors can open security holes and compromise the effectiveness of encryption. Therefore, it is important to follow programming best practices and take rigorous measures to test and verify the algorithm implementation. Another key aspect in symmetric cryptography is key management. It is essential to use secure algorithms for key generation and to adopt robust protocols for key distribution, storage and updating. Loss or compromise of the secret key could lead to a breach of the encrypted data. Symmetric encryption offers an effective solution to ensure data confidentiality, using a shared secret key to encrypt and decrypt information. Symmetric encryption algorithms, such as AES, DES, 3DES, Blowfish, and Twofish, offer a variety of options to fit your specific security needs. However, it is critical to understand that the security of symmetric encryption depends on proper key management and robustness of the implementation. Secure key generation, secure key distribution, and key management are all critical to ensuring the security of your encrypted data. Symmetric encryption, when used correctly, can offer adequate data protection against external threats. However, it is important to take into account security best practices and system-specific considerations to ensure adequate protection.

Asymmetric encryption algorithms

Asymmetric cryptography is a cryptographic approach that uses two distinct keys: a public key and a private key. This system offers numerous advantages over symmetric encryption, such as secure communications over insecure channels and simplified key management. A widely used algorithm in asymmetric cryptography is RSA (Rivest-Shamir-Adleman). RSA exploits the computational difficulty of factoring large prime numbers to ensure communications security. The sender uses the recipient's public key to encrypt messages, which can only be decrypted using the corresponding private key. In addition to the RSA algorithm, there are other important asymmetric encryption algorithms. An example is the ElGamal algorithm, based on the discrete logarithm problem. ElGamal is used for data encryption and also offers digital signature and secret key sharing capabilities. Another common cryptographic technique is the Diffie-Hellman key exchange algorithm. This algorithm allows two entities to establish a shared session key over an insecure communication channel. Diffie-Hellman plays a crucial role in ensuring the confidentiality of communications and is often used in combination with other cryptographic algorithms. Key management is a fundamental aspect of asymmetric cryptography. Each entity involved in the process must have a key pair: a public key and a private key. The public key is distributed widely, while the private key must remain secret and protected. One of the challenges in key management is authenticating a recipient's public key. There are several techniques, such as certifying keys via certificate authorities (CA) and using digital signatures, to ensure that the public key actually belongs to the intended recipient. Despite the security offered by asymmetric encryption, there are some potential threats. For example, an attacker might try to crack a private key using efficient discrete logarithm or factorization techniques. To mitigate such threats, it is critical to use keys of adequate length and robust algorithms. Successfully implementing asymmetric encryption requires attention to several aspects. It is crucial to use reliable cryptographic algorithms and libraries and regularly check for vulnerabilities and security updates. Additionally, it's a good idea to follow key management best practices, such as random key generation, properly protecting private keys, and using secure key lengths and algorithms. A successful implementation of asymmetric encryption also requires consideration of aspects such as performance and efficiency, especially in large communication scenarios. By continuing to maintain a good understanding of the principles and techniques of asymmetric cryptography, you can use this advanced form of encryption to ensure secure communications and protect sensitive data.

Public key encryption and private key encryption

Public key cryptography and private key cryptography are two fundamental approaches in modern cryptography. These cryptographic systems offer solutions for communications security and sensitive data protection, but they use different approaches to achieve their goals. Private key encryption, also known as symmetric encryption, involves using the same key to encrypt and decrypt data. The key is kept secret and known only by the parties involved in the communication. This system is known for its speed and efficiency, but presents a significant challenge in securely distributing the key itself. Public key cryptography, on the other hand, involves the use of a pair of keys: a public key and a private key. The public key is accessible to everyone, while the private key is kept secret by the owning entity. The sender uses the recipient's public key to encrypt the data, which can only be decrypted using the corresponding private key. Private key cryptography is widely used for symmetric cryptographic operations, such as protecting data on a hard drive or encrypting an Internet connection. Some well-known algorithms for private key encryption include AES (Advanced Encryption Standard), DES (Data Encryption Standard), and 3DES (Triple Data Encryption Standard). On the other hand, public key cryptography is often used for encrypting communications over insecure channels and for purposes such as digital signature and secure key exchange. Popular algorithms for public key cryptography include RSA, Diffie-Hellman, and ElGamal. Private key encryption offers greater speed and efficiency than public key encryption. Furthermore, the encryption and decryption process is relatively simple, requiring fewer computational resources. However, one of the main disadvantages of private key cryptography is the need to share the key securely between the parties involved. On the other hand, public key cryptography eliminates the need to secretly share the key, making the process more secure and convenient. Furthermore, it offers additional features such as digital signature and secure key exchange. However, public key cryptography is generally slower and requires more computational resources than private key cryptography. Private key cryptography is commonly used in applications that require a high degree of speed and efficiency, such as encrypting data on storage devices or securing Internet connections via protocols such as SSL/TLS. On the other hand, public key cryptography is widely used in scenarios where it is necessary to ensure the security of communications over insecure channels. It is used for email encryption, digitally signing documents, protecting data during online transactions, and secure key exchange for private key cryptography. Public key cryptography and private key cryptography are two fundamental concepts of modern cryptography. Both offer solutions for communications security and sensitive data protection, but use different approaches to achieve their goals. Private key cryptography is fast and efficient, but requires secure key distribution. Public key cryptography eliminates this challenge by allowing encryption and decryption using a pair of public and private keys. However, public key cryptography is generally slower and requires more computational resources. Both cryptosystems have specific applications in different contexts and offer unique advantages. The choice between public key cryptography and private key cryptography depends on your specific application needs and security considerations. Understanding the differences and applications of both forms of encryption is essential to successful cybersecurity implementation.

Correct use of encryption to protect sensitive data

The protection of sensitive data has become a critical element in the digital context in which we live. With the increase in cyber threats and security breaches, it is critical to use encryption correctly to ensure data confidentiality, integrity and availability. Proper use of encryption involves applying reliable cryptographic algorithms and implementing proper key management. In this section, we will explore the fundamental principles for the correct use of encryption to protect sensitive data. Choosing the right cryptographic algorithms is a fundamental aspect of ensuring the security of sensitive data. Symmetric and asymmetric cryptographic algorithms are two main categories used to protect data. Symmetric cryptographic algorithms use the same key to encrypt and decrypt data. Some common examples of symmetric cryptographic algorithms include AES (Advanced Encryption Standard) and DES (Data Encryption Standard). These algorithms are known for their efficiency and speed, making them suitable for encrypting large amounts of data. On the other hand, asymmetric cryptographic algorithms use a key pair: a public key to encrypt data and a corresponding private key to decrypt it. RSA (Rivest-Shamir-Adleman) and ECC (Elliptic Curve Cryptography) are examples of widely used asymmetric cryptographic algorithms. These algorithms are known for their robustness and are often used for operations such as digital signature and key exchange. The choice of cryptographic algorithms should be based on their security, compatibility with industry standards and their suitability for specific data protection needs. Encryption key management is a crucial element of correctly using encryption to protect sensitive data. Encryption keys play a vital role in the process of encrypting and decrypting data, and their correct management is essential to avoid unauthorized access and ensure data integrity.

Key management includes several activities, including:

1. Secure key generation: Keys must be generated using reliable cryptographic algorithms and secure procedures to ensure their randomness and resistance to guessing.

2. Secure Key Distribution: Keys must be securely transferred to authorized parties without compromising their confidentiality. Techniques such as Diffie-Hellman key exchange and key distribution via secure channels can be used to ensure security in key distribution.
3. Secure key storage: Keys must be stored securely to protect them from unauthorized access. Using hardware cryptographic modules (HSM) or key management software (KMS) can help ensure key security.
4. Periodic key rotation: Keys should be regularly replaced with new keys to mitigate the risk of long-term key compromise.
5. Revocation of Compromised Keys: If a key is compromised or suspected of being compromised, it must be revoked and replaced with a new key.

Proper management of encryption keys is essential to ensuring the safety of sensitive data and preventing security breaches. Protecting sensitive data often requires applying encryption at multiple levels. This means that sensitive data must be protected not only during transmission, but also during storage and processing. During transmission, data can be protected using cryptographic protocols such as SSL/TLS. These protocols encrypt data during communication between the client and server, ensuring that data is protected from eavesdropping and manipulation by unauthorized third parties. When storing data, file-level or disk-level encryption can be used to protect sensitive data. File-level encryption encrypts individual files, while disk-level encryption encrypts the entire disk or partition where the data is stored. This ensures that your data is protected in the event of unauthorized physical access to your storage device. Additionally, field- or record-level encryption can be used to protect sensitive data within applications. This form of encryption encrypts specific fields or records within the database, allowing only authorized users to access sensitive data. Implementing encryption at different levels of sensitive data requires careful analysis of security requirements and applying the correct encryption techniques based on your specific needs. Proper use of encryption is critical to protecting sensitive data. Choosing the correct cryptographic algorithms, properly managing encryption keys, and applying encryption to different layers of sensitive data are all key to ensuring data security. However, it is important to note that encryption alone is not enough to ensure complete protection. Encryption should be integrated into a broad security strategy that also includes physical protection, authentication, authorization and monitoring measures. In conclusion, the correct use of cryptography to protect sensitive data requires a thorough understanding of cryptographic principles, choosing the appropriate algorithms, and correct key management. Only through rigorous implementation of encryption and the integration of complementary security measures will it be possible to ensure the protection of sensitive data in the digital age.

Network Security
Basic concepts of networks and communication protocols

In this section, we will explore the basic concepts of networks and communication protocols. We'll start with an overview of computer networks, including the most common network types such as LAN, WAN, and WLAN. Next, we'll look at fundamental communications protocols, such as TCP/IP and the OSI model, that provide the foundation for exchanging information between network devices. We will also delve into the different network technologies, such as Ethernet and Wi-Fi, and their main characteristics. We continue our exploration of networks by focusing on network topologies and network architectures. Network topologies define how network devices are connected to each other and can be star, mesh, ring, tree, etc. We wil examine the characteristics of each topology and the associated advantages and disadvantages. Next, we will discuss different network architectures, such as client-server and peer-to-peer, and their specific applications. On the third page of this section, we will delve deeper into routing and switching protocols, which play a crucial role in transporting data within networks. We will look at the most common routing protocols, such as OSPF and BGP, and their routing algorithms used to determine the best paths to send data packets. Additionally, we'll explore switching protocols, such as STP and VLAN, that allow you to route data between network devices efficiently and securely. Let's now move on to the aspect of network security. We will discuss major threats and common attacks that can compromise network security, such as data interception, packet injection, phishing, and denial of service (DoS). Next, we will explore the security technologies and techniques used to protect networks from such threats. This will include the use of firewalls, VPN (Virtual Private Network), IDS (Intrusion Detection System) and IPS (Intrusion Prevention System). We conclude this section with an overview of best practices for protecting networks. We'll discuss network segmentation strategies, which help you separate internal networks from external ones and limit access to sensitive data. We will also examine the importance of regularly updating network devices with the latest security patches to mitigate vulnerabilities. Finally, we will talk about the importance of user training and awareness to create a security culture in organizations.

Common threats and attacks on networks

Computer networks are exposed to a wide range of threats and attacks that can compromise the security of data and communications. Understanding these threats and how to protect networks is essential to ensuring the security of sensitive information. In this section, we will explore some of the common network threats and attacks. We'll start with an overview of threat types, including network vulnerabilities, malware, unauthorized access, and denial of service (DoS) attacks. Next, we'll delve into the details of each threat, analyzing the techniques attackers use and the goals they pursue. Computer networks are subject to several vulnerabilities that attackers can exploit to compromise security. Some of the key network vulnerabilities include lack of strong authentication, inadequate permission management, insecure default configurations, and vulnerabilities in communication protocols.

To mitigate these vulnerabilities and protect your network, it is critical to take a variety of security measures. Here are some tips to protect your network from these vulnerabilities:

1. Implement strong authentication: Ensure that all users accessing the network undergo proper authentication. This may include using strong passwords, two-factor authentication, or using digital certificates.
2. Proper permission management: Assign users appropriate privileges based on their responsibilities and limit access to only necessary resources. It is advisable to follow the "principle of least privilege" principle, granting only essential permissions to do your job.
3. Secure Configurations: Avoid using the default configurations provided by network devices, as they are often known to attackers. Securely configure network devices, including routers, switches, and firewalls, using unique passwords, enabling encryption, and disabling unnecessary features.
4. Regularly update devices: Keep your network devices updated with the latest updates and security patches. This includes both the operating system

and the firmware of the network devices. Updates often fix known vulnerabilities and improve overall system security.
5. Using Firewalls: Configure and use firewalls to filter unwanted network traffic. Firewalls can block unauthorized access attempts and prevent malware from spreading across your network. Make sure your firewall is configured correctly and that your filtering rules are up to date.
6. Data encryption: Use encryption to protect sensitive data that is transmitted over the network. Encryption makes data unreadable to anyone without the correct key. Encryption protocols such as SSL/TLS can be used to ensure secure communications. Network traffic monitoring: Implement network traffic monitoring tools to detect suspicious or anomalous activity. These tools can help identify potential network attacks and intrusions.
7. Security Awareness: Provide cybersecurity training and awareness to network users. Users should be educated on good security practices, such as avoiding clicking on suspicious links or attachments, using strong passwords, and reporting suspicious activity.

By implementing these security measures, you can significantly reduce network vulnerabilities and protect your network from malicious attacks. It is important to maintain a robust and up-to-date security policy to address ever-evolving threats. In the world of cybersecurity, there are numerous types of attacks that aim to compromise the security of networks. Understanding these threats is essential to taking effective protective measures. Below are some of the common types of network attacks:
1. Eavesdropping Attacks: These attacks involve an attacker's interception of network traffic in order to obtain sensitive information. Interception can occur through methods such as network sniffing or the use of malicious software. Attackers can obtain login credentials, personal data, or sensitive company information.
2. Spoofing Attacks: Spoofing attacks occur when an attacker impersonates another legitimate entity or network device. A common example is IP address

"spoofing", in which an attacker changes the source IP address of a network packet to hide their identity or deceive recipients.

3. Denial-of-service (DoS) attacks: These attacks aim to overload a network or service with an excessive volume of requests, making it inaccessible to legitimate users. DoS attacks can be performed using botnets, packet floods, or by exploiting specific system vulnerabilities.

4. Man-in-the-middle (MITM) attacks: In a MITM attack, the attacker positions himself between two communicating parties, intercepting and manipulating communications between them. This allows the attacker to obtain sensitive information or alter transmitted data without the parties involved realizing it.

5. Phishing Attacks: Phishing is a type of attack in which attackers send fake messages or websites that appear to come from trusted sources in order to trick people into providing personal information, such as usernames, passwords, or financial details. Phishing can be done via email, text messages, phone calls, or social media.

6. Ransomware Attacks: Ransomware is a type of malware that blocks access to an organization's data or systems, demanding a ransom to restore access. These attacks can cause serious damage to corporate networks and sensitive data.

7. Password cracking attacks: Attackers can attempt to crack passwords to access networks using techniques such as brute force attacks or using common password dictionaries. Once they have the passwords, they can access the network and sensitive data.

8. Social Engineering Attacks: Social engineering involves the psychological manipulation of people to gain unauthorized access to networks or sensitive information. Attackers can use persuasion or manipulation tactics to trick people into revealing sensitive information or performing malicious actions.

It is important to understand these types of attacks and how they occur in order to take appropriate security measures to protect your networks. In the next section, we will review the tools and techniques available for protecting networks against such attacks.

Tools and techniques for protecting networks

Securing networks is a constant challenge due to the increase in cyber threats. To defend networks from malicious attacks, it is essential to adopt appropriate security tools and techniques. In this section, we will explore in detail some of the most effective solutions for protecting networks from internal and external threats. A fundamental component of network security is the firewall. This tool acts as a barrier between the internal network and the outside world, filtering network traffic based on predefined rules. The firewall can be configured to block unauthorized or dangerous data packets, thus reducing the risk of intrusions or unauthorized access. Additionally, it can be set to only allow certain types of traffic, such as VPN connections, which provides greater security in data transmission. Another common security technique for networks is the Intrusion Detection System (IDS), which monitors network traffic for anomalies or suspicious activity. This system can detect potential attacks or security breaches and generate alerts for network administrators to take appropriate action. The IDS can be configured to detect unusual traffic patterns, unauthorized access attempts, or anomalous activity in system logs. In addition to IDS, IPS (Intrusion Prevention System) provides an additional layer of security for networks. Unlike IDS, IPS is not limited to just detecting threats but takes active actions to prevent them. Using predefined security rules or machine learning algorithms, IPS can block malicious traffic or unauthorized access, thus preventing attacks from succeeding. IPS can be integrated with your firewall to provide more comprehensive and dynamic network protection. A critical aspect of network security is the management of devices and user permissions. Lack of strong authentication or inadequate permission management can create vulnerabilities in your network. It is important to have a strong authentication and access management policy in place to ensure that only authorized users can access data and network resources. This can be accomplished by implementing mechanisms such as two-factor authentication, which requires the use of two distinct elements to log in, such as a password and a temporary code sent to the user's smartphone. To protect Wi-Fi networks from unauthorized access, you should use security protocols such as WPA2 (Wi-Fi Protected Access 2). These protocols encrypt wireless network traffic to prevent sensitive information from being intercepted by third parties. Furthermore, it is advisable to set up Wi-Fi networks with strong passwords and change them regularly to avoid unauthorized access. Finally, it is important to take into account the evolution of cyber threats and available security solutions. New attacks and vulnerabilities are discovered regularly, so it is crucial to monitor security updates and patches provided by network device and software manufacturers. Furthermore, it is advisable to constantly monitor your network and update security measures as threats and attacks evolve. Securing networks requires a holistic approach and a combination of security tools, techniques and policies. Implementing firewalls, IDS, IPS and robust authentication solutions are only part of the measures needed to ensure a secure network. It is essential to create a culture of security and adopt good network management practices to ensure that cyber threats are addressed effectively and promptly. Vulnerabilities in communication protocols are another critical point to consider when protecting networks. Many protocols, such as the File Transfer Protocol (FTP) and the Telnet protocol, transmit data in the clear without encryption, making it vulnerable to interception and manipulation. We recommend using secure communication protocols, such as SSH (Secure Shell) and HTTPS (Hypertext Transfer Protocol Secure), which encrypt network traffic to ensure data confidentiality and integrity. Another common attack on networks is Denial of Service (DoS), which aims to overload the network or network services, making them inaccessible to legitimate users. There are various forms of DoS attacks, such as sending massive data packets to the network, excessive consumption of system resources, or interference with communication protocols. To protect networks from DoS attacks, solutions such as Distributed Denial of Service (DDoS) mitigation systems can be implemented, which monitor network traffic and block malicious packets from suspicious IP addresses. Another common threat is wireless security breach. Wi-Fi networks can be vulnerable to several forms of attacks, such as traffic interception, unauthorized access, and spoofing the network's identity. To protect wireless networks, it is important to use security protocols such as WPA2, which offer strong encryption and user authentication. Additionally, you should disable network name (SSID) broadcasting to make your network less visible to attackers and limit access to only authorized devices using Media Access Control (MAC) filters. To protect networks from attacks from insiders, strong security policies must be implemented. This includes limiting user privileges, adopting strong authentication mechanisms, and segregating network segments to limit access to critical resources. Additionally, training users on cybersecurity best practices is essential to fostering a culture of security and preventing errors or unsafe behavior. In conclusion, protecting networks requires a comprehensive approach that includes security tools, techniques and policies. Understanding common network threats and attacks is critical to taking appropriate preventative measures. The implementation of firewalls, IDS, IPS, secure communication protocols and effective security policies helps mitigate risks and ensure the protection of corporate networks. However, network security is an ever-evolving process, requiring constant monitoring, updates and adaptations to address increasingly sophisticated and rapidly evolving cyber threats. In addition to common network threats and attacks, it is critical to understand defense techniques and best practices to ensure the security of corporate networks. One of the most effective solutions for protecting networks is the use of firewalls. A firewall is a device or software that monitors network traffic and applies security rules to control access to network resources. There are hardware and software firewalls, which can be placed at the network perimeter level or at the individual device level. Firewalls can filter traffic based on IP addresses, communication ports, protocols, and other criteria, allowing only authorized traffic and blocking unwanted or potentially harmful traffic. It is important to properly configure firewalls and keep security rules up to date to ensure adequate protection. Another important tool for protecting networks is the IDS (Intrusion Detection System) and the IPS (Intrusion Prevention System). The IDS constantly monitors network traffic for suspicious activity or anomalies that could indicate an intrusion attempt. When potentially malicious activity is detected, the IDS generates alerts for network administrators, allowing them to take action. IPS, however, goes beyond simple detection and can take automatic actions to prevent or block ongoing attacks, for example by blocking the sender's IP address. Deploying IDS and IPS enables timely response to attacks and increased network security. Network segmentation is another important practice for corporate network security. Segmentation involves dividing the network into separate logical or physical segments, based on criteria such as department, function, or data sensitivity. This limits the spread of any attacks and makes it easier to control and manage access to network resources. Segmentation can be achieved through the use of separate Virtual Local Area Networks (VLANs) or subnets, and can be implemented with the help of firewalls or advanced network switches. Another crucial aspect for network security is the management of updates and patches. Software vendors regularly release updates that fix vulnerabilities and security holes in their software. It is critical that enterprise networks have an effective update management process in place, including identifying required patches, assessing the impact on existing systems, testing patches before deployment, and applying updates in a timely manner critics. Failure to update systems can leave networks vulnerable to known attacks and exploit unpatched vulnerabilities. In conclusion, network protection is a fundamental aspect of cybersecurity. Understanding common network threats and attacks, as well as implementing the right defense measures, is essential to ensuring the security of business information and systems. The use of firewalls, IDS, IPS, network segmentation and effective update management are just some of the strategies that can be adopted to protect networks. However, it is important to underline that network security is an ongoing and evolving process, requiring the constant attention of network administrators and the adoption of up-to-date security practices and technologies.

Firewall, IDS and IPS

Firewalls, IDS (Intrusion Detection System) and IPS (Intrusion Prevention System) are essential tools for protecting corporate networks and mitigating cyber threats. Each of them plays a specific role in network security and work synergistically to ensure effective protection. The firewall is a security barrier that filters incoming and outgoing network traffic, controlling and managing access to network resources. It works based on a set of rules configured by the network administrator, which determine which network packets can pass through the firewall and which are blocked. It can be implemented as a dedicated hardware device or as software installed on a system. Firewall configuration rules can be based on IP addresses, communication ports, protocols, and other specific criteria. It can also provide Network Address Translation (NAT) capabilities to hide the network's internal IP addresses and provide an additional layer of protection. The IDS (Intrusion Detection System) is a system that actively monitors network traffic for suspicious activity or anomalous behavior that could indicate an intrusion attempt or an attack in progress. It uses a variety of techniques to identify threats, such as pattern-based signature, anomaly analysis, and inspection of network packet contents. When potentially malicious activity is detected, the IDS generates an alert or notification to the network administrator, who can then take appropriate measures to mitigate the attack. It can be implemented as a stand-alone system or as an integral part of a firewall or larger security system. The IPS (Intrusion Prevention System) is closely related to the IDS and is designed to go beyond simple intrusion detection, taking immediate action to prevent and block ongoing attacks. It uses information collected by the IDS to identify threats and can take automatic steps to mitigate them, such as blocking traffic from a suspicious IP address or dropping a malicious connection. It can be implemented as a stand-alone system or as an integral part of a firewall or integrated security system. The combined use of firewalls, IDS and IPS allows for more robust and complete protection of corporate networks. The firewall acts as a first line of defense, filtering unauthorized or potentially harmful traffic. The

IDS actively monitors network traffic for anomalous activity and generates alerts for the network administrator. IPS goes beyond IDS by taking immediate measures to prevent and stop ongoing attacks. Together, these tools provide a multi-layered defense that protects corporate networks from internal and external threats. It is important to note that the correct configuration and management of these tools is critical to their effectiveness. Network administrators must define and maintain appropriate firewall configuration rules, carefully monitor alerts generated by the IDS, and promptly respond to threats detected by the IPS. Additionally, regular firmware and security signature updates are essential to keep systems aligned with the latest threats and vulnerabilities. Firewalls are essential components of network security and can be divided into several categories, each with their own characteristics and functionality. One of the most common types is the state-based firewall, which operates at the network layer and tracks the state of network connections. This type of firewall can determine whether a packet is part of an established connection, whether it is legitimate, and whether it should be allowed or blocked based on predefined security rules. Some firewalls include packet filtering capabilities, which allow you to control traffic based on information contained in packet headers, such as source and destination IP addresses, communication ports, and protocols used. These firewalls can block or allow packets based on filtering rules defined by the network administrator. Another type of firewall is the application firewall, which operates at the application level. This type of firewall can inspect traffic based on the specific protocols and services used. For example, it can analyze HTTP traffic for potential threats such as cross-site scripting (XSS) or SQL injection attacks. The application firewall can also allow or block specific types of application traffic, such as accessing certain websites or sending certain types of files. When it comes to configuring firewalls, it is essential to define a clear security strategy. This involves creating filtering rules based on company policies, such as only allowing certain IP addresses or communication ports. Network segmentation can also be implemented through the firewall, creating logical zones or segments with specific filtering rules. This can help limit the propagation of any attacks within the network. It is also important to constantly monitor firewall activity by logging and analyzing security logs. This allows you to identify suspicious activity or attempted breaches and take timely action. Additionally, regular firmware and security definition updates are essential to keep your firewall up to date with the latest threats and vulnerabilities. When it comes to choosing a firewall, there are several options on the market. It is advisable to opt for reliable and proven security solutions offered by well-known and reputable vendors. However, the choice of firewall also depends on your specific business needs and requirements. It is important to consider characteristics such as management capabilities, reliability, performance and scalability of the firewall. Firewalls are fundamental tools for protecting corporate networks and computer systems. The most common types of firewalls include network firewalls, application-level firewalls, and cloud-based firewalls. Each type offers specific benefits and requires proper configuration to ensure adequate protection. Network firewalls operate at the network layer, allowing or blocking traffic based on filtering rules based on IP addresses, ports, and protocols. They can also include network address translation (NAT) capabilities to mask internal IP addresses. Setting up a network firewall requires a thorough understanding of your organization's security policies. You need to define specific traffic rules based on your business needs. Application layer firewalls operate at a higher level than network firewalls. They analyze application traffic in detail, including data contained in packets, and make filtering decisions based on application specifications. Configuring an application-level firewall requires defining rules that allow or block traffic based on application protocols and services. For example, you can create rules to allow HTTP and HTTPS traffic, while blocking insecure Telnet or FTP traffic. As the adoption of cloud services increases, cloud-based firewalls are becoming increasingly important. These firewalls provide centralized protection for cloud resources and network traffic between on-premises networks and cloud resources. Setting up a cloud-based firewall involves defining specific security policies to protect your cloud resources. For example, you can create rules to only allow access to cloud resources from authorized IP addresses or use advanced security services offered by cloud providers. Correct configuration of firewalls is essential to ensure their effectiveness. In addition to establishing appropriate filtering rules, it is important to constantly monitor firewall activity, analyze security logs, and maintain firmware updates. Additionally, working with security experts can be helpful in ensuring proper firewall configuration and adopting best security practices. IDSs are security tools that actively monitor network traffic or system logs to identify and report suspicious activity or attempted intrusions. Their main objective is to detect and promptly respond to intrusions or security breaches in the company network. There are different types of IDS, including signature-based IDS, anomaly-based IDS and hybrid IDS that combine both techniques. Signature-based IDSs use a database of predefined signatures to detect intrusions. These signatures are known attack patterns or patterns, which are compared against network traffic or system logs to identify matches. If a match is detected, the IDS generates an alert or report to the network administrator. Signature-based IDSs are effective at detecting known attacks, but may struggle to detect new attack variants or zero-day attacks. Anomaly-based IDSs constantly monitor network traffic or system logs to identify anomalous behavior. This type of IDS creates a profile of normal network or system behavior and compares observed activities to the profile to identify anomalies. For example, if a user starts generating a much higher volume of traffic than usual, an anomaly may be reported. Anomaly-based IDSs can be more effective at detecting unknown or novel attacks, but they can also generate more false positives. Hybrid IDSs combine signature and anomaly techniques to provide more comprehensive protection. These IDSs use both the signature database to detect known attacks and anomaly analysis to identify anomalous behavior that may indicate new threats. The combined use of both techniques allows for greater precision in intrusion detection. Correct configuration and management of IDSs are critical to their effectiveness. IDSs must be properly configured to detect and report intrusions without generating a high number of false positives or false negatives. This requires a thorough understanding of the organization's security policies and relevant threats. Network administrators must define configuration rules that reflect the specific needs of the organization and must be able to correctly interpret alerts generated by IDSs. Additionally, it is important to regularly analyze IDS security logs to identify any suspicious activity or attack trends. Integrating IDS with other security tools, such as firewalls, can increase the overall effectiveness of network defense. It is also advisable to keep IDSs updated with the latest attack signatures or anomalous behavior patterns, as threats constantly evolve over time. Regular software and firmware updates to IDSs are essential to ensure they are able to detect the latest threats. Finally, it is important to underline that IDSs are detection tools, but not prevention tools. If suspicious activity or an attempted intrusion is detected, appropriate response measures must be taken to mitigate the threat. This could include isolating the compromised system, disconnecting it from the network, or initiating a forensic investigation to determine the extent of the attack and the impact on the organization's security. IPS are advanced security tools that go beyond simple intrusion detection, as they are designed to actively prevent attacks and mitigate their effects. Unlike IDSs, which simply detect and report intrusions, IPSs can take immediate action to block or mitigate detected threats. IPS uses a combination of techniques, such as signature-based detection, anomaly-based detection, and behavior-based detection, to identify attacks and take necessary countermeasures. Signature-based detection is similar to that used in IDS. IPSs have a database of predefined signatures that are compared against network traffic or system logs for matches to known attacks. When a match is detected, the IPS can take immediate action to block the malicious traffic, such as cutting the connection or blocking the suspicious IP address. Anomaly-based detection monitors network traffic or system logs to identify anomalous behavior. IPSs create a profile of normal network or system behavior and constantly compare observed activities to the profile. If a significant anomaly is detected, the IPS can take actions to prevent the attack or mitigate its effects. Behavior-based detection is a more advanced technique that involves analyzing system and user behavior to identify potential malicious activity. IPS constantly monitor network traffic and system behavior to detect patterns of suspicious or unauthorized activity. When malicious behavior is detected, the IPS can take actions to block or limit the malicious activity. IPSs are often implemented as network security devices, placed between the internal and external networks, to monitor and filter incoming and outgoing traffic. This strategic positioning allows IPS to immediately block attack attempts or malicious activity before they reach internal systems. As with IDSs, the correct configuration and management of

IPSs are critical to their effectiveness. Network administrators must define configuration rules that reflect the specific needs of the organization and must be able to correctly interpret the alerts generated by IPS. Additionally, IPSs must be regularly updated with the latest attack signatures and behavior patterns to ensure adequate protection against emerging threats.

APPLICATION SECURITY
Main vulnerabilities in software applications

In the context of software application security, it is essential to understand the main vulnerabilities that can compromise their integrity and security. These vulnerabilities can be exploited by attackers to gain unauthorized access to systems, execute malicious code, or access sensitive information. Let's look at some of the main software application vulnerabilities and how the associated risks can be mitigated. A major vulnerability plaguing many applications is code injection. This type of vulnerability occurs when an application accepts invalidated or insufficiently filtered input from the user and uses it directly in its code or in database queries. Attackers can exploit this vulnerability to inject malicious code or alter queries, allowing them to gain unauthorized access to data or perform unauthorized operations. To mitigate this risk, it is critical that applications implement proper validation and sanitization of user input, for example using query parameterization or special character escape mechanisms. Another common vulnerability is Cross-Site Scripting (XSS). This vulnerability occurs when an application does not properly filter user-provided data and allows malicious script execution on pages viewed by other users. Attackers can exploit this vulnerability to steal user login information, modify page content, or perform malicious actions. To mitigate the risk of XSS, applications must implement proper validation and sanitization of incoming data and use methods such as HTML entity tagging to avoid unwanted script execution. Vulnerabilities related to authentication and authorization are also a significant concern. Applications often require users to authenticate to access resources or perform certain actions. However, poor authentication management can allow attackers to bypass controls and gain unauthorized access to data or application functionality. Additionally, insufficient privilege control can allow users to perform actions that they should not be allowed to do. To mitigate these vulnerabilities, it is critical to adopt strong authentication practices, such as the use of strong passwords and proper session management, and implement strong authorization controls to limit access to resources to only authorized users. Session management is another critical area where vulnerabilities can emerge. Applications often use sessions to maintain user state during a browsing session. However, poor session management can allow attackers to steal or manipulate legitimate users' sessions. This could allow the attacker to impersonate an authenticated user or acquire sensitive information. To mitigate this risk, applications should implement secure session management, such as using strong session tokens, periodic session renewals, and secure storage of authentication information. Exploits are tools or techniques used by attackers to exploit vulnerabilities in systems or applications to gain unauthorized access or execute malicious code. Exploits exploit specific weaknesses in the software or protocols used by systems to breach their security. To find exploits, security experts take several approaches. One of the common methods is vulnerability analysis. Security analysts carefully examine the software, source code and protocols used, in order to identify potential vulnerabilities that could be exploited by attackers. This may involve using automated tools or manually inspecting the code. Another method used to find exploits is scanning for vulnerabilities. Security experts actively perform testing and analysis to find new vulnerabilities before they are discovered by attackers. This may involve creating specific test scenarios to explore software behavior or analyzing network communications for weaknesses. Additionally, security experts may consider information from external sources, such as security announcements released by software vendors or vulnerability reports from the security community. This information can provide insights into new vulnerabilities or exploits discovered. Once a vulnerability is identified, security experts work to develop an exploit that exploits that specific weakness. This may involve analyzing the internal workings of the software, identifying the conditions necessary to exploit the vulnerability, and developing code or a command sequence that allows it to be exploited. Importantly, security experts also work to mitigate the vulnerabilities found by communicating them to software vendors and developers so that they can be fixed through the application of security patches or software updates. In conclusion, exploits are tools or techniques used by attackers to exploit vulnerabilities in systems or applications. Security experts use various methods, such as vulnerability analysis, vulnerability research, and analysis of information from external sources, to identify and understand existing vulnerabilities. They then develop exploits to exploit these vulnerabilities and work to mitigate risks by communicating discovered vulnerabilities to software developers and vendors.

Application testing to identify security flaws

When it comes to finding software security flaws, cybersecurity professionals use a number of specialized tools. These tools are designed to identify vulnerabilities and weaknesses in applications, operating systems, and networks. Let's look at some of these software and how they can be used effectively. A widely used software for vulnerability scanning is Nessus. This comprehensive tool allows you to scan networks, operating systems and applications to identify known vulnerabilities. Before using Nessus, it is important to understand its features and set it up correctly. For example, it is advisable to set the scan target specifically, specifying the IP addresses or domain names to scan. Additionally, you can customize scanning options as needed, such as selecting specific vulnerability categories to scan or setting the risk level for vulnerability assessment. Once the scan is complete, Nessus provides a detailed report with the vulnerabilities found, classified by severity. It is important to carefully analyze the results and take the necessary measures to fix the identified vulnerabilities. A widely used tool for web application penetration testing is Burp Suite. It is a set of tools that allow you to perform a series of security tests on web applications. Burp Suite's main feature is its web proxy, which allows you to intercept and manipulate HTTP traffic between your browser and the web application under consideration. This allows security analysts to perform attacks such as code injection, manipulation of input parameters, and exploration of application resources. In addition to the web proxy, Burp Suite offers other useful features. For example, it includes a vulnerability scanner that automatically scans your application for known vulnerabilities. This tool identifies and reports vulnerabilities such as cross-site scripting (XSS), SQL injection, remote file inclusion (RFI), and others. Additionally, Burp Suite has an automated intrusion module that allows you to automate attacks and exploit detected vulnerabilities. To use Burp Suite effectively, it is important to acquire skills in penetration testing and attack techniques specific to web applications. You need to understand the context of the application you are testing, common vulnerabilities in web applications, and best practices for remediating identified vulnerabilities. Another tool used in web application penetration testing is OWASP ZAP. ZAP is open source software developed by the Open Web Application Security Project (OWASP). It offers similar features to Burp Suite, such as web proxy for interception and manipulation of HTTP traffic, vulnerability scanner, and other useful features for analyzing web applications. One of ZAP's defining features is its community orientation and open source approach. This means that ZAP is developed by the community and fosters collaboration and knowledge sharing in vulnerability research. Users can contribute to the project, develop new modules and report discovered vulnerabilities. As with Burp Suite, it is important to gain knowledge about web application vulnerabilities, such as injection, cross-site scripting (XSS), and others, as well as associated attack techniques to use ZAP effectively. You must carefully configure ZAP to adapt it to the specific needs of the application you are testing. Regarding tools used for writing exploits, it is crucial to highlight that the use of such tools for illegal purposes or without the consent of the owner of the system or application is strictly prohibited. However, understanding how these tools work can be helpful in understanding vulnerabilities and developing effective countermeasures. Metasploit is one of the best-known tools for penetration testing and exploit development. It is a framework that offers a wide range of tools, modules and vulnerability databases to perform controlled penetration testing. Metasploit can be used to explore known vulnerabilities in the target system, exploit these vulnerabilities and gain unauthorized access to the system. Its tools also allow you to test security defenses and develop solutions to mitigate discovered vulnerabilities. Importantly, using Metasploit requires advanced technical skills and in-depth knowledge of target systems and networks. It is essential to obtain appropriate consent before using Metasploit and to act in accordance with laws and company policies. Similarly, Nmap (Network Mapper) is a widely used tool for scanning networks. Allows you to discover hosts, open ports, and services running on a network. Nmap can help identify potential entry points and vulnerabilities in your network configuration. For example, it can reveal unnecessary open ports, outdated services with known vulnerabilities, or insecure network configurations. The security analyst can then use this information to take action and mitigate the identified vulnerabilities. Finally, Wireshark is a network packet analysis tool that allows you to capture and analyze network traffic in real time. Wireshark can be used to identify potential security issues, such as transmitting sensitive data in the clear or spotting suspicious activity on the network. For example, it can help identify man-in-the-middle attacks, where an attacker intercepts and manipulates network traffic between two parties. To use Wireshark effectively, you must understand network protocols, such as TCP/IP, and have a good understanding of packet analysis techniques. Wireshark is a powerful but complex tool, requiring technical expertise to correctly interpret the captured data and detect potential security issues. It is important to emphasize that the use of these tools should always be done in an ethical and legal manner. They should only be used with appropriate consent and in compliance with laws and company policies.

Best practices for developing secure applications

When it comes to secure application development, it is critical to follow best practices to ensure data protection and overall application security. Applications can be vulnerable to various vulnerabilities, such as injections, cross-site scripting (XSS), insecure input processing, and others. Here are some basic principles for developing secure applications. First, one of the key best practices is accurate validation of input data. It is essential to verify and sanitize data that is provided by users or other external sources before using it in your application. This can be done using validation and sanitization functions provided by development libraries or frameworks, such as the htmlspecialchars() function in PHP to prevent XSS attacks. Another crucial aspect is the adoption of secure password management. User passwords should be stored in encrypted form, preferably using secure hashing algorithms such as bcrypt or Argon2. Additionally, it is a good idea to impose complexity requirements for passwords, such as minimum length, the use of special characters, and the combination of uppercase and lowercase letters. Two-factor authentication (2FA) can further strengthen password security. Privileged access to application resources must be carefully managed. Permissions should be assigned based on the principle of least privilege, where users only get the permissions they need to perform their specific tasks. Additionally, it is important to implement robust authentication and authorization mechanisms to ensure that only authorized users can access sensitive resources. Protecting sensitive data is a critical aspect of developing secure applications. Sensitive information, such as personal data or user passwords, must be stored securely. It is advisable to use strong encryption algorithms to encrypt sensitive data during storage and during transmission across insecure networks, for example using the HTTPS protocol for web communications. Regularly updating the libraries and frameworks used in your application is another important practice. Vulnerabilities are constantly being discovered, and library developers frequently release patches and updates to address such issues. Ensuring you always use the latest versions of libraries and frameworks and apply security updates is critical to mitigating known vulnerabilities. Additionally, it is a good idea to implement protection against brute force attacks and unauthorized access attempts. Limit the number of login attempts allowed, for example by using temporary account lockout mechanisms after a certain number of failed attempts. Additionally, it is important to log and monitor login and authentication events to detect any suspicious activity. In addition to error handling, it is important to consider protection against client-side scripting attacks. A common attack is cross-site scripting (XSS), in which an attacker inserts malicious code into web pages viewed by other users. To prevent XSS attacks, you need to implement proper escaping of your output strings and sanitize your data appropriately. Using libraries or frameworks that offer automatic escaping capabilities, such as AngularJS or React, can make this task much easier. Another crucial aspect is protection against injection vulnerabilities, such as SQL injections and command injections. These vulnerabilities occur when input data is not properly validated and used directly in database queries or system commands. It is critical to use prepared query parameters or parametric declarations to avoid inserting malicious code into your SQL queries. Additionally, when executing system commands, you should use functions or libraries that allow you to pass parameters safely, avoiding concatenation of command strings. Secure session management is another critical aspect of developing secure applications. Sessions should be managed securely, and session tokens should be randomly generated, resistant to guesswork, and expire after an appropriate amount of time. Furthermore, it is advisable to use secure cookies and protect sessions from attacks such as session fixation and session hijacking. Using strong authentication mechanisms, such as JSON Web Tokens (JWT) or server-based sessions, can help ensure session security. In the context of web applications, communications security is a critical factor to consider. The adoption of secure communication protocols such as HTTPS (HTTP over SSL/TLS) is essential to protect data during transmission. Using valid SSL/TLS certificates, enabling transport-level encryption, and properly configuring web servers are important aspects of ensuring secure communication between your application and users. Furthermore, it is crucial to implement the principle of defense in depth. This means that security should not depend on a single security measure, but should be based on a set of multiple security controls. For example, in addition to authentication and authorization, you should implement application-level access control mechanisms, such as role and permission management. This allows you to limit access to application data and features to authorized users only. Last but not least, it is crucial to keep the application updated. Security vulnerabilities can be discovered in the software used by the application, such as third-party libraries, frameworks, or components. Ensuring you apply security updates and patches promptly helps mitigate the risks associated with these vulnerabilities. Additionally, it is advisable to regularly conduct security tests, such as penetration testing and vulnerability analysis, to identify and resolve any security holes in your application's code or configuration. In conclusion, developing secure applications requires the adoption of several best practices. From error handling to protection against injection vulnerabilities, from proper string escaping to implementing robust authentication mechanisms, these practices are critical to ensuring application security. Remember that security should be considered early in development and maintained as an ongoing process to mitigate the ever-present threats in today's digital environment.

Patch and update management

Patch and update management is a crucial aspect of ensuring the security of software applications. Vulnerabilities can emerge due to programming errors, security flaws in the software used, or new threats discovered by developers. Attackers exploit these vulnerabilities to infiltrate applications and gain unauthorized access to sensitive data or damage the system. For effective patch management, you need to take a systematic and proactive approach. First, it is important to regularly monitor security advisories released by software vendors and organizations responsible for cybersecurity. These alerts provide crucial information about newly discovered vulnerabilities and available fixes. Once you have identified the necessary patches, it is critical to carefully evaluate them before applying them to your production environment. This evaluation may include compatibility testing to verify that patches do not cause malfunctions or incompatibilities with the application or other system components. It is also a good idea to perform a risk analysis to evaluate the impact of the patches on the functionality and security of the application. This preliminary assessment phase ensures that patches are applied appropriately and reduces the risk of outages or residual vulnerabilities. A critical element of patch management is timely software updates. Software vendors regularly release security patches to address known vulnerabilities. These patches must be applied without delay to keep the application protected from evolving threats. Delays in patching can leave your application exposed to significant risks, especially if vulnerabilities are publicly available or actively exploited by attackers. It is important to have a clear policy for patch management, establishing defined response times for applying fixes. This may include scheduling regular maintenance windows dedicated to installing patches. Furthermore, it is advisable to automate the patch management process to ensure efficient management and minimize human errors. There are patch management solutions that help you automatically identify and apply relevant patches based on your application-specific configurations and dependencies. Another important aspect of patch management is managing third-party dependencies. Modern applications often use third-party libraries, frameworks, and components to speed up development. However, these dependencies can be vulnerable to cyber threats. You must maintain an updated list of all third-party dependencies used in your application and monitor update and patch releases for these components. Vulnerabilities discovered in third-party dependencies should be addressed immediately through the application of vendor-provided patches. Additionally, patch and update management requires close collaboration between developers and system administrators. Developers should be aware of best practices for secure development and include patch management early in application development. It is advisable to provide training and awareness to developers on security threats and the importance of timely patching. Finally, patch and update management should not be viewed as a one-time activity, but as an ongoing process. Cyber threats evolve rapidly, and vulnerabilities can emerge at any time. It is therefore essential to maintain a constant monitoring and review program to identify new vulnerabilities and respond promptly through the application of appropriate patches. This preventative and proactive approach is essential to keeping applications secure over time. However, patch and update management alone is not enough to ensure the complete security of an application. A number of best practices must be adopted to effectively develop and maintain secure applications. First, it is critical that developers adopt a security by design approach early in application development. This means that security must be integrated into the development process itself, rather than being an afterthought. Developers should be trained in secure development best practices, such as validating and sanitizing input data, securely managing credentials, and implementing appropriate security controls. Additionally, it is essential that developers conduct a careful analysis of security requirements during the application design phase. This involves identifying and evaluating potential risks and threats that the application may face. Security requirements analysis helps define application security objectives and establish appropriate protection measures. During application development, it is important to implement robust security controls to protect the application from common attacks, such as code injection, insecure data processing, and sensitive information disclosure. Using secure development frameworks and applying secure development best practices, such as privilege separation and data validation, are critical to reducing application vulnerabilities. Additionally, developers need to be aware of the most common security vulnerabilities plaguing applications and new threats that are constantly emerging. Participating in developer communities, reading specialized blogs and articles, and attending cybersecurity conferences can help developers stay up to date on the latest security trends and practices. Another critical aspect for the development of secure applications is the correct management of permissions and access. Developers must implement an access management system that assigns appropriate privileges to users based on their responsibilities and limits access to only necessary features and data. Permissions management must be periodically reviewed and updated to accommodate changes in the system and ensure that users do not have unauthorized access. In addition to patch and update management, another important application security practice is using regular security testing. Security testing, such as penetration testing and vulnerability testing, helps you identify and fix vulnerabilities before they are exploited by potential attackers. It is advisable to conduct security tests at all stages of application development, as well as during its operation. It is also crucial to adopt a strong and secure password management policy. Weak or easily guessable passwords represent a significant vulnerability for applications. Developers should promote the use of strong passwords and encourage users to use multi-factor authentication methods to increase the security of their credentials. Finally, it is crucial that developers constantly monitor applications for any suspicious activity or unauthorized access attempts. The implementation of logging and monitoring mechanisms for application activities allows you to promptly identify any violations or anomalies in the application's behavior. In conclusion, best practices for developing secure applications require a holistic approach that includes patch and update management, secure development by design, analysis of security requirements, implementation of robust security controls, permission management, regular security testing, a strong password management policy and constant application monitoring. These practices, when adopted in a consistent and integrated manner, can help mitigate vulnerabilities and protect applications from cyber threats.

DATA PROTECTION
Basic principles of data protection

Data protection is a fundamental aspect in the digital age we live in. Chapter 5 addresses the basic principles that guide data protection, providing a solid foundation for securely managing sensitive information. The first key principle of data protection is the concept of confidentiality. This means that personal data must be treated confidentially and accessible only to authorized persons. It is critical to implement appropriate security measures, such as the use of strong authentication and data encryption, to ensure that your personal information is protected from unauthorized access. Another important principle is that of data integrity. This means that data must be accurate, complete and reliable throughout its lifecycle. To ensure data integrity, you must take protective measures such as validation checks, change logs, and regular backup procedures. The third principle is data availability. Authorized users must be able to access data when they need it. This requires implementing secure storage solutions, planning for business continuity and managing vulnerabilities that could compromise access to data. Data minimization is another important principle for data protection. It means that only data necessary to achieve a specific purpose should be collected and stored. Reducing the amount of personal data also reduces the risk of unauthorized access and possible breaches. Another key principle is limiting data retention. Personal data should only be kept for as long as necessary to achieve the purpose for which it was collected, and then it should be securely deleted. Data retention and deletion must be handled in accordance with applicable laws and regulations. Finally, the principle of accountability is crucial in data protection. Organizations must take responsibility for protecting the personal data they collect and process. This includes adopting appropriate policies and procedures, training staff on data protection and designating data protection officers to ensure compliance with privacy laws and regulations. Managing personal data requires a holistic approach that embraces the principles of confidentiality, integrity, availability, data minimization, retention limitation and accountability. First, to ensure data confidentiality, authentication and authorization mechanisms must be implemented. Users must be securely authenticated before they can access data, and assigned appropriate authorization levels based on their responsibilities and the purposes of data processing. Furthermore, data encryption is a key measure to ensure confidentiality. Encryption makes data unreadable to anyone who does not have the correct decryption key, thus protecting personal information from unauthorized access. It is important to use strong encryption algorithms and keep encryption keys securely. Regarding data integrity, validation controls must be implemented to ensure that data is accurate and complete. This may include verifying data formats, validating digital signatures, and verifying relationships between data. Additionally, it is important to maintain change logs to track any changes made to the data and ensure its integrity over time. To ensure data availability, measures must be taken to protect against data loss and service interruptions. This includes business continuity planning, creating backup copies of your data, and implementing redundant storage solutions. In the event of an incident or failure, it is important to be able to quickly restore access to data to avoid prolonged disruptions to operations. Data minimization means that only strictly necessary data should be collected and stored. Before collecting any personal data, you should carefully evaluate the purpose of the processing and determine what information is actually necessary to achieve that purpose. Reducing the amount of data collected also reduces the risk of unauthorized access and possible security breaches. Limiting data retention is closely linked to data minimization. Personal data should only be kept for as long as necessary to achieve the purpose for which it was collected, unless it is required for legal or regulatory purposes. It is important to establish clear policies and procedures for data retention and ensure that it is securely deleted when it is no longer needed. Finally, data protection responsibility requires a commitment from organizations to adopt adequate policies and procedures. It is important to designate data protection officers who are responsible for ensuring compliance with privacy laws and regulations. Furthermore, it is essential to provide training and awareness on good data management practices to all staff involved in processing personal information. In conclusion, basic data protection principles, including confidentiality, integrity, availability, data minimization, retention limitation, and liability, are critical to ensuring secure handling of personal data and protecting individuals' privacy. The application of these principles requires a holistic approach involving the implementation of appropriate technical, organizational and procedural measures. This holistic approach to data protection also implies the need for a risk assessment. Every organization must conduct a thorough risk assessment to identify potential threats to personal data and evaluate the impact such threats could have on individuals' privacy. This risk assessment helps determine the appropriate security measures to implement and take a proportionate approach to data protection. Furthermore, transparency is a key element in data protection. Organizations must be transparent about their data handling practices and privacy policies. It is necessary to provide individuals with clear and understandable information about the collection, use, storage and sharing of their personal data. This can be achieved through the adoption of well-written privacy policies, the creation of privacy notices and the implementation of procedures for the exercise of individuals' rights regarding their data. Another fundamental aspect is data access control. It is important to ensure that only authorized persons have access to personal data and that this access is limited to the specific purposes for which it was granted. This can be achieved through the implementation of authentication mechanisms, the assignment of access rights based on the need-to-know principle and the monitoring of access to sensitive data. Data protection also requires careful management of security breaches. Organizations must develop breach response plans that include clear procedures for breach notification, root cause investigation, containment and recovery of operations. It is critical to respond promptly to breaches to mitigate potential harm and restore individuals' trust in the protection of their personal data. Finally, organizations must be aware of evolving privacy laws and regulations and must adapt accordingly. It is important to monitor new regulations and adapt your data management practices to ensure compliance. This may require updating policies and procedures, implementing new security measures and training staff on new regulatory requirements. In conclusion, data protection is a crucial area to ensure the privacy and security of personal information. The application of basic data protection principles, such as confidentiality, integrity, availability, data minimization, retention limitation and liability, together with the implementation of appropriate technical, organizational and procedural measures, helps to create a secure environment for management of personal data. Organizations must take a holistic approach to data protection, considering all aspects of personal data management, from policies and procedures to infrastructure security and breach management. Furthermore, compliance with privacy laws and regulations is an essential element to ensure data protection effectively.

Data encryption techniques

Data encryption is one of the main techniques used to ensure the protection of personal data. Cryptography is the application of complex mathematical algorithms to transform data into an unreadable form, called ciphertext, which can only be read by those who have the correct decryption key. Data encryption offers an additional layer of security, as even if an attacker manages to access the encrypted data, they will not be able to understand it without the correct key. This ensures the confidentiality and integrity of the data, protecting it from unauthorized access and fraud. There are several encryption techniques used to protect data. One of the most common techniques is symmetric key cryptography, where the same key is used to encrypt and decrypt data. This type of encryption is fast and efficient, but requires the key to be shared between the parties involved. Another technique is asymmetric key cryptography, which uses a pair of keys: a public key to encrypt data and a private key to decrypt it. The public key is available to everyone, while the private key is strictly guarded by the owner. This system allows secure communication between parties, without the need to share the same key. Additionally, there are cryptographic hash algorithms that are used to verify the integrity of data. Hashing algorithms transform data into a fixed-length string, called a hash, that represents a unique fingerprint of the original data. Any changes to the data will cause a completely different hash, allowing any unauthorized alterations to be detected. Importantly, data encryption should be used in conjunction with other security measures to ensure complete protection. For example, it is critical to implement secure key management mechanisms to prevent encryption keys from falling into the wrong hands. Additionally, the use of security protocols, such as the SSL/TLS protocol for Internet communication, helps ensure that data is transmitted securely across insecure networks. It helps ensure that data is transmitted securely across insecure networks. The SSL/TLS (Secure Sockets Layer/Transport Layer Security) protocol is widely used to establish secure connections on the Internet. This protocol uses a combination of symmetric and asymmetric encryption to secure communications between a client and a server. When a client connects to a server via SSL/TLS, a "handshake" process occurs that includes exchanging cryptographic keys and verifying the server's authenticity. During this phase, a secure session is established and a unique "session key" is generated to encrypt and decrypt the data transmitted between the two parties. Encrypting data during transmission is essential to prevent any interception by ill-intentioned third parties. Through the use of strong cryptographic algorithms, the data is rendered incomprehensible to anyone who does not have the correct key to decrypt it. In addition to encryption during transmission, it is essential to also consider encryption of data at rest. This refers to protecting data when it is stored on storage devices, such as hard drives or servers. Using appropriate encryption algorithms, data is encrypted before being stored and can only be decrypted with the correct key. There are several widely used cryptographic algorithms, such as Advanced Encryption Standard (AES), Triple Data Encryption Standard (3DES), and RSA. These algorithms have undergone extensive review and are considered safe when used correctly. However, it is important to note that encryption security also depends on proper key management. Encryption keys must be created securely, stored appropriately, and given only to authorized individuals. Loss or compromise of encryption keys could compromise data security. Furthermore, data encryption must be integrated into a broader framework of security measures, such as protecting systems from cyber attacks, training staff on data security and complying with personal data protection regulations. In conclusion, data encryption techniques play a vital role in protecting personal data both during transmission and while it is stored. Encryption ensures the confidentiality and integrity of the data, preventing unauthorized third parties from accessing or manipulating it. However, it is crucial to implement these techniques correctly and adopt a comprehensive security strategy to protect sensitive data from potential threats.

Data backup and restore

Data backup and recovery are two fundamental aspects of data protection. Creating regular data backups and the ability to restore them in the event of loss or corruption are essential practices to ensure business continuity and information security. Data backup involves creating copies of data at a specific point in time and storing them in a secure location. This helps protect your data from unexpected events, such as hardware failure, human error, cyber attacks, or natural disasters. Backups can be made to physical media, such as external hard drives or tapes, or to digital media, such as cloud storage services. It is important to establish a backup strategy that defines the frequency of backups, the data to include and the storage method. Backups can be scheduled to run regularly, such as daily, weekly, or monthly, depending on your organization's needs. Additionally, we recommend performing full backups and differential or incremental backups to optimize storage space and recovery time. In addition to regularly creating backups, it is equally important to periodically test your data recovery process. An ineffective backup or poorly configured restore process could render its existence useless. Running recovery tests on a test environment or virtual machine can help verify the integrity of your backups and the correctness of your recovery procedures. The choice of backup method depends on the specific needs of your organization. Some prefer backups to physical media, which offer more direct control over the data stored. However, physical media can be subject to failure, damage, or theft. In contrast, backing up to cloud storage services offers a cost-effective and scalable option, but requires a reliable internet connection and data encryption solutions to ensure data security. An important aspect of data backup is keeping backups in a secure location separate from your organization's main office. This protects the data from any incidents that might affect the building or surrounding area. For example, backups can be stored at a disaster recovery site or in a cloud storage service with geographically distributed data centers. In addition to regular backups, it is also advisable to implement a data versioning policy. Versioning allows you to maintain several copies of your data over time, allowing you to recover previous versions of your files should the need arise. This practice is useful for handling errors or unwanted changes and can be especially important for shared files or collaborative projects. In conclusion, data backup and recovery are critical to the protection and security of your business information. Regularly creating backups and verifying the recovery process helps ensure data availability in the event of data loss, failure, or breach. Choosing the right backup method, keeping backups in a secure location, and implementing a data versioning policy are all important practices to ensure business continuity and the protection of sensitive information. In addition to regularly backing up your data, it is equally important to consider the retention period of your backups. The duration for which backups are stored depends on your organization's needs and applicable regulations. Some industries, such as finance or healthcare, may have specific requirements regarding retaining backup data for a certain period of time. It is important to ensure the integrity of your backups throughout their entire lifecycle. This involves protecting backups from unauthorized modifications, ensuring that they are always accessible and that the data they contain is correct and complete. Using data encryption methods can be an effective solution to protecting the integrity of your backups. Encryption allows you to encode data in such a way that it is readable only by those who have the correct decryption key. Additionally, it is important to take into account the geographic location of your backups. If your organization operates in multiple jurisdictions or countries, you should evaluate local privacy laws and regulations regarding data transfer and retention. This may include data sovereignty and regulatory compliance considerations. In addition to data backup, it is essential to have a well-defined data recovery strategy. This strategy should include both file- and system-level recovery plans. File-level recovery helps you recover specific files or data, while system-level recovery aims to restore your entire working environment, including the operating system, applications, and data. To ensure that your data recovery process is effective, it is a good idea to document the steps required to perform the recovery and identify the necessary resources, such as hardware, software, or storage media. It is also a good idea to designate personnel responsible for data recovery and ensure they have the skills and knowledge needed to manage the process. Finally, it is important to periodically test your data recovery procedure. This helps identify any problems or gaps in the process and allows any improvements to be made. Recovery tests can be conducted on a dedicated test environment or on a virtual machine, so as not to compromise the production environment. In summary, data backup and recovery are critical to ensuring business continuity and the protection of company information. Regular backup creation, data integrity, backup security, a well-defined recovery strategy and periodic testing are key elements of a solid data backup and recovery strategy. In addition to the fundamental concepts of data backup and recovery, there are some additional practices that can help improve the robustness and effectiveness of these operations. A best practice is to adopt a backup versioning policy. Versioning allows you to maintain multiple copies of your data over time, allowing you to restore a specific version of your files or data. This is especially useful in case data corruption or accidental alteration occurs. Storing different versions of your backups can allow you to recover older data without losing the most recent changes. Additionally, it is important to consider diversifying your backups. This involves using different backup and storage solutions, such as disk backup, tape backup, cloud backup, or a combination of these options. Diversifying your backups helps mitigate risks associated with hardware failure, human error, or natural disasters. If you have problems with one backup option, you can rely on another to restore your data. Another aspect to consider is automating data backup and recovery processes. Automation allows you to schedule and run regular backups automatically, minimizing the need for human intervention and the risk of errors. This ensures that backups are always up-to-date and complete, without having to depend on manual user action. Finally, it is essential to ensure the security of the backups themselves. Backups contain sensitive and confidential data and must be protected like any other company data. This involves implementing security measures, such as encryption of backups, both during transfer and during storage. Encryption ensures that data is inaccessible to unauthorized third parties, even if backups are compromised or lost. In conclusion, data backup and recovery requires a holistic strategy that includes regular backup creation, data integrity, a versioning policy, backup diversification, process automation, and security of archived data. These practices help ensure the availability, integrity and confidentiality of company information, playing a critical role in data protection and business continuity of the organization. To ensure the effectiveness of data backup and recovery, it is also important to conduct regular tests and audits. Backup tests help you evaluate the integrity of your backups and your ability to restore data should the need arise. It is advisable to carry out periodic tests to check whether backups are working and whether data can be restored correctly. This helps identify any problems or gaps in the backup and recovery process, allowing you to make any necessary improvements. Additionally, it is essential to establish a documented procedure for data recovery. This procedure should include detailed instructions on how to successfully restore data from different backup sources. It is important that the personnel responsible for data recovery are adequately trained and aware of the procedure to follow. In disaster situations, having a documented procedure can help reduce downtime and quickly restore critical data to your organization. In addition to data backup and recovery, it is equally important to consider long-term storage. Some information may need to be retained for long periods of time to comply with regulatory or legal requirements. You need to identify which data requires long-term retention and adopt an appropriate archiving strategy to ensure data integrity and accessibility over time. This may include using specific storage technologies or implementing storage solutions that can handle large volumes of data over the long term. Finally, it's important to periodically evaluate your overall data backup and recovery strategy to ensure it's aligned with your evolving business needs. Backup technologies and solutions are advancing rapidly, requiring constant attention to adopting best practices and new technologies available. Additionally, it is critical to take into account changes in regulatory and legal compliance requirements that may impact data backup and recovery policies. In conclusion, data backup and recovery are critical processes to ensure the protection and availability of company information. Proper planning, automation, diversification of backups, regular testing, a documented recovery procedure and constant evaluation of the strategy are all key elements of effective data management. Investing in data protection and recovery can reduce the risks of data loss, ensure business continuity and maintain customer trust. To ensure reliable data backup and recovery, it is essential to also consider the security of your backup copies. Sensitive and critical data should be encrypted during the backup process to protect it from unauthorized access. The use of robust encryption algorithms and the adoption of good key management practices are essential to ensure the confidentiality and integrity of data during its transfer and storage. Additionally, it is important to carefully consider the storage location of your backups. Ideally, backups should be stored in a location geographically distant from primary systems. This offers additional protection in the event of catastrophic events such as fires, floods, or other incidents that could physically damage the data production environment. Choosing a safe and reliable location for storing backups reduces the risk of total data loss in the event of an accident. Another crucial aspect of managing backups is maintaining multiple versions of your data. Sometimes it may be necessary to restore a previous version of a file or an entire database due to human errors, cyber attacks, or other unexpected situations. Maintaining multiple copies of your backups incrementally or differentially can allow you to recover specific versions of your data as needed. Additionally, it is important to establish a backup retention policy that dictates how long different versions of data should be retained for compliance or historical purposes. A crucial element to ensuring successful data recovery is carefully documenting all procedures. Every step of the data backup and recovery process should be recorded and documented in detail. This includes information such as the date and time of the backup, the backup mode used, the type of data covered, verification procedures, and the recovery method. Complete, up-to-date documentation saves valuable time in the event of an emergency and ensures that data recovery personnel are able to follow the correct procedures. Finally, don't forget proactive backup monitoring and management. It is essential to implement a monitoring system that monitors the integrity of backups, the performance of storage devices and the outcome of recovery tests. In this way, you can promptly detect any problems or malfunctions in the data backup and recovery process and take the necessary corrective measures. In conclusion, data backup and recovery is a critical element in protecting business information. Adopting good practices, such as data encryption, choosing a secure storage location, maintaining multiple versions of backups, and carefully documenting procedures, help ensure effective data management. Proactively monitoring and managing backups helps you identify issues early and maintain the integrity of your critical data. Investing in the right data backup and recovery solutions is a crucial investment for security and business continuity.

Management of access to sensitive data

Managing access to sensitive data is a crucial aspect of protecting corporate information. To ensure the security and confidentiality of sensitive data, a series of measures must be taken to control access and limit the privileges of users and systems. One of the first actions to take is to implement a robust authentication system. This may include using strong passwords, multi-factor authentication, biometrics, or other advanced methods to ensure only authorized users can access sensitive data. It is important to educate users about creating and managing passwords securely, encouraging the use of unique passwords and changing them regularly. Furthermore, it is essential to define and enforce an access control policy. This policy should identify who has the right to access sensitive data and define access levels based on job responsibilities. We recommend using role and privilege management to ensure that users only have the access they need to perform their tasks, thus avoiding the proliferation of excessive privileges. Another important aspect is the segregation of duties. Separating responsibilities between different users or teams reduces the risk of accidental abuse or breaches. For example, teams that handle sensitive data should not have access to login credentials or administration functions for that data. Maintaining a clear separation of responsibilities helps mitigate the risks associated with unauthorized access. Regularly reviewing access is another best practice to ensure that users maintain only the access privileges they need. Access to sensitive data should be evaluated periodically and revoked or modified based on the user's work needs. This review can be supported by access management tools and access logs, which provide a detailed overview of user activities and changes to access privileges. In parallel, it is essential to establish rigorous device and network management policies. This includes placing restrictions on external access to sensitive data, using virtual private networks (VPNs) for remote connections, and implementing encryption tools to protect data transmission across insecure networks. Finally, it is important to provide ongoing cybersecurity training to everyone in your organization. Raising staff awareness of the risks associated with unauthorized access, misuse of sensitive data and cyber threats helps create a security culture where data protection is considered a shared responsibility. In conclusion, managing access to sensitive data requires a combination of policies, procedures and tools to ensure that only authorized users have access to sensitive information. Implementing robust authentication measures, establishing access control policies, segregating duties, reviewing access, and providing cybersecurity training are just some of the best practices to protect sensitive data and prevent security breaches. Another important aspect in managing access to sensitive data is the implementation of monitoring and anomaly detection mechanisms. These tools help you identify suspicious or unusual activity, such as unauthorized access attempts or anomalous user behavior. Monitoring systems can generate real-time alerts to enable immediate action and prevent potential security breaches. Furthermore, it is essential to adopt a mobile device and personal device management (BYOD, Bring Your Own Device) policy. This policy defines the rules and restrictions for the use of mobile devices within the organization and establishes the security measures necessary to protect sensitive data accessed through such devices. This may include installing mobile device management software, encrypting data, separating business data from personal data, and enforcing specific access and security policies. Additionally, it is important to establish security protocols for managing passwords. This may include implementing password expiration policies, requiring strong passwords, and using password management tools to ensure credentials are protected and managed securely. Managing access to sensitive data also requires close collaboration with the system administration team and IT staff. It is important to ensure that security controls are properly implemented, configured and monitored to ensure data protection. This may include implementing firewalls, intrusion detection systems, data loss prevention systems and other security solutions to protect sensitive data from unauthorized access or accidental loss. Finally, it is critical to maintain a culture of safety within your organization. This means promoting the importance of protecting sensitive data, encouraging reporting of potential vulnerabilities or security incidents, and providing ongoing training on cybersecurity best practices. In conclusion, managing access to sensitive data requires a combination of policies, procedures, tools and collaboration between different actors within the organization. By implementing robust authentication measures, activity monitoring, device and password management policies, collaborating with your IT team and promoting a security culture, you can effectively protect sensitive data and mitigate the risk of security breaches. Continuing with managing access to sensitive data, another crucial aspect is implementing appropriate authorization controls. This means that not all users need to have full access to all sensitive data in the organization. Roles and access privileges must be defined based on each user's responsibilities and work needs. For example, a human resources employee might only have access to employee data, while a system administrator might have access to organization-wide data. Authorization controls can be implemented through the use of Access Management Systems that allow you to define and apply granular access policies. These systems allow you to centrally manage user access privileges, ensuring that only authorized people can access sensitive data. Another important aspect is the recording of user activities. Logging user activities allows you to track who accesses sensitive data, when and what they do with it. This is useful for identifying and analyzing any suspicious or unauthorized activity. In the event of a security incident, activity logging can provide useful evidence for the investigation and resolution of the issue. It is equally crucial to consider managing access privileges in the context of organizational changes, such as employee hiring, promotions, or terminations. It is critical to revoke or update the access privileges of employees who leave the organization or change roles within it. Additionally, you need to ensure that new employees receive the appropriate access privileges based on their responsibilities. It is important to highlight the importance of physical security when managing access to sensitive data. While much data is stored digitally, it is essential to also protect the physical devices that contain that data, such as servers, storage devices, or backup media. It is necessary to ensure that these devices are placed in secure areas, accessible only to authorized personnel and protected by physical security measures, such as keys, biometric access or video surveillance systems. Finally, it is essential to regularly audit and review access controls to ensure their effectiveness and compliance with security policies. This may include analyzing access logs, evaluat ng authorization policies, identifying potential vulnerabilities or gaps in existing controls, and updating security measures as necessary. In conclusion, managing access to sensitive data requires implementing appropriate authorization controls, logging user activity, managing access privileges based on orgar izational changes, physically securing devices, and performing regular audits. Only by adopting a holistic approach to access management can you ensure the protection of sensitive data and mitigate the risks of security breaches.

MANAGEMENT OF THREATS AND SECURITY INCIDENTS
Monitoring and detection of cyber threats

Cyber threat monitoring and detection are essential processes for protecting sensitive data and ensuring information security within an organization. These processes focus on early identification of suspicious activities, unauthorized intrusions and anomalous behavior that could pose a threat to data security. To implement an effective cyber threat monitoring and detection system, it is necessary to use a combination of technological tools and advanced analysis approaches. These tools can include intrusion detection systems (IDS), advanced threat detection systems (ATD), security information and event management systems (SIEM), and user behavioral analytics (UBA). Intrusion Detection Systems (IDS) are designed to monitor network traffic in real time to detect potential intrusions or anomalous activity. These systems can be signature-based, recognizing known patterns of attacks, or behavior-based, detecting anomalies compared to normal network usage patterns. The IDS can provide immediate alerts or generate detailed reports that allow network administrators to take action. Advanced Threat Detection (ATD) systems go beyond traditional IDS, using algorithms and machine learning techniques to detect unknown or sophisticated threats. These systems analyze file behavior, network traffic, and other parameters to detect suspicious activity. ATD can detect emerging attack patterns or advanced evasion techniques that may elude traditional security systems. Security information and event management (SIEM) systems are designed to collect, correlate, and analyze security logs from different sources, such as servers, network devices, applications, and operating systems. These systems allow you to identify patterns of anomalous or potentially malicious activity through the centralized analysis of security data. SIEM provides a comprehensive view of network activities and possible security incidents, facilitating immediate response to critical events. User behavioral analysis (UBA) is an approach that focuses on monitoring user behavior within a system or application to identify unusual activity or behavior that is out of the ordinary. This type of analysis can detect unauthorized access, fraudulent access attempts, or anomalous behavior that could be indicative of a security breach. UBA is based on identifying patterns of normal behavior and alerting when significant deviations from those patterns occur. In today's environment, organizations are constantly exposed to a wide range of cyber threats, such as cyber attacks, malware, phishing and data breaches. To protect your systems and data, it is critical to implement a robust threat detection and monitoring system. Cyber threat monitoring involves constantly observing and analyzing security events to identify potential suspicious or anomalous activity. There are several techniques and tools used for monitoring, including:

1. Log monitoring: Security logs generated by systems and applications are analyzed for signs of unauthorized activity or anomalous behavior. This may include analysis of access logs, security event logs, and transaction logs.
2. Network Monitoring: Network monitoring devices are used to analyze network traffic in real time to detect suspicious activity. These devices can identify traffic anomalies, unauthorized access attempts or communications to suspicious IP addresses.
3. Behavioral analysis: The behavioral analysis technique is based on the creation of behavioral profiles of systems and authorized users. Any significant deviation from normal behavior patterns may indicate a potential attack or data compromise.

Once a threat or suspicious activity is identified, threat detection allows you to take immediate action to prevent further damage. Some common detection methods include:

1. Alarms and notifications: Security systems can generate alarms or notifications when suspicious activity is detected. These notifications are sent to security administrators or monitors to take appropriate action.
2. Signature Analysis: Known attack or malware signatures are used to identify matches in files, network packets, or system activity. When a match is detected, an alarm is generated.

3. Heuristic analysis: Heuristic analysis focuses on detecting common attack behaviors or patterns, rather than specific signatures. This method can spot suspicious activity even if it doesn't match known attack signatures.

Furthermore, the use of advanced technologies such as artificial intelligence and machine learning can significantly improve the ability to monitor and detect cyber threats in a timely and effective manner. These technologies can analyze large amounts of data in real time and identify patterns and anomalies that are difficult to detect manually. Monitoring and detecting cyber threats is an ongoing and evolving process. It is important to keep monitoring systems and tools up to date and adapt them to new emerging threats. Furthermore, good communication and collaboration between the security team and internal and external stakeholders are essential to ensure a rapid and effective response to threats. When it comes to managing cybersecurity threats and incidents, it is crucial to have a robust cyber threat monitoring and detection system. This process allows for early detection of any suspicious activity or anomalies in the organization's systems and networks, enabling a rapid response and mitigating potential damage. Cyber threat monitoring involves constantly observing your organization's IT environment to identify unwanted or potentially malicious activity. This may include analyzing system logs, observing network traffic, monitoring user activity, and using intrusion detection systems (IDS) or security information management (SIEM) tools. . A key part of cyber threat monitoring is identifying anomalies. This involves analyzing patterns of normal behavior of systems and users, so that we can detect any deviations that could indicate an attack or suspicious activity. For example, an abnormal increase in network traffic to a particular server or unauthorized access to a system could be signs of a potential attack. To detect these anomalies, advanced tools and technologies are needed to analyze large amounts of data in real time and apply threat detection algorithms. Artificial intelligence and machine learning can be used to identify patterns and trends that indicate a potential attack or anomalous behavior. Once a threat has been identified, it is important to implement a rapid and effective response. This may include isolating compromised systems, disabling compromised user accounts, or applying security patches to mitigate the exploited vulnerability. In some cases, it may also be necessary to involve law enforcement or external consultants to address more complex threats. In addition to monitoring and detecting cyber threats, it is critical to develop and test security incident response plans. These plans should include clear procedures for incident management, assignment of responsibility, guidelines for incident reporting, evidence collection and post-incident analysis. In conclusion, managing cybersecurity threats and incidents requires a strategic and proactive approach. Monitoring and detecting cyber threats allows you to identify attacks early and take the necessary countermeasures to protect your organization's data and systems. Additionally, it is important to have well-defined incident response plans to effectively address security events and minimize negative impacts

Security incident response

Security incident response is a critical component of managing cyber threats. It involves identifying, managing and resolving any security breaches that may occur within an organization. When a security incident occurs, it is essential to act promptly to limit the damage and restore the security of your data and systems. Security incident response includes several phases, each of which plays an important role in the incident management process. The first phase consists of preparation. This phase involves developing detailed incident management plans and procedures, identifying necessary resources, and training staff on actions to take in the event of an incident. It is important that your organization has a documented and regularly updated incident response plan, so that you are ready to react in a timely and effective manner. The second phase is the detection and evaluation of incidents. In this phase, monitoring systems and threat detection tools are used to identify ongoing security incidents. It is important that your organization has real-time incident detection mechanisms, so it can respond quickly to potential breaches. Once an incident has been detected, the actual response phase is initiated. This phase involves implementing the necessary actions to mitigate the incident and restore safety. These actions may include isolating compromised systems, disabling compromised user accounts, applying security patches, or restoring data from secure backups. It is important that the organization has a dedicated security incident response team, with clearly defined roles and responsibilities. Once the incident has been managed and resolved, the post-incident analysis phase begins. In this phase, the organization evaluates the incident, identifies the underlying causes, and develops corrective measures to prevent future similar incidents. Post-incident analysis may include reviewing security logs, examining system vulnerabilities, and updating security policies and procedures. Finally, there is the continuous learning and improvement phase. Managing security incidents provides a valuable opportunity to learn and improve your organization's security capabilities. It is important that the organization conducts a regular review of its incident response processes, identifies areas for improvement and implements necessary corrective actions. Once the incident has been managed and resolved, the organization enters the post-incident analysis phase. This phase is of fundamental importance because it allows you to fully understand the incident, identify the underlying causes and develop corrective measures to prevent future similar incidents. During post-incident analysis, your organization can review security logs to gain insights into the incident. Log analysis can reveal the events that led to the incident, the actions taken by the attackers, and the system vulnerabilities that were exploited. This information is critical to understanding how the incident occurred and to identifying any weaknesses that need to be addressed. Additionally, during post-incident analysis, it is important to examine system vulnerabilities that contributed to the incident. This may include identifying missing or outdated security patches, system misconfigurations, or human error. Identifying these vulnerabilities allows the organization to take steps to mitigate them and strengthen the overall security of the system. Another crucial aspect of post-incident analysis is the examination of the organization's security policies and procedures. It is important to evaluate whether existing policies were adequate to prevent the incident and whether safety procedures were followed correctly. If weaknesses or gaps in policies and procedures are identified, the necessary changes must be made to ensure greater security. Post-incident analysis is not only limited to identifying causes and vulnerabilities, but also to developing corrective measures. Based on the lessons learned from the incident, the organization can define targeted corrective actions to prevent future similar incidents. These corrective measures may include updating security policies, reviewing access management processes, implementing additional controls, or providing additional training for staff. Finally, managing security incidents provides an opportunity for continuous learning and improvement for the organization. It is essential that the organization conducts regular reviews of its incident response processes, identifies areas for improvement and implements necessary corrective actions. This approach allows the organization to constantly strengthen its security and adapt to new emerging threats. In conclusion, security incident management requires a comprehensive approach that goes beyond immediate incident response.

Post-incident analysis and corrective measures are critical to understanding the underlying causes of the incident, preventing future incidents, and improving the overall safety of the organization. Continue to invest in the resources and expertise needed to handle security incidents in a timely and effective manner, and you will be able to protect the integrity and confidentiality of your data.

Continuity planning and post-incident recovery

Continuity planning and post-incident recovery are two key components to ensuring operational resilience and business recovery following a security incident. These processes enable the organization to mitigate the adverse effects of the incident, restore systems and services, and resume normal operations as quickly as possible. Continuity planning refers to the creation of strategies and plans that enable the organization to maintain or restore its critical functions during or after an incident. This phase involves identifying the processes and services essential to the functioning of the organization, as well as identifying the resources necessary to support these activities in the event of an interruption. Continuity planning can include implementing backup infrastructure, duplicating critical systems, and establishing emergency procedures. Once the incident has been managed and resolved, post-incident recovery focuses on recovering the data, systems and services compromised during the incident. This process involves applying recovery procedures and restoring the IT environment to previous configurations. It is important that your organization has up-to-date, secure backups of critical data to enable rapid recovery. Additionally, verification and testing activities may be necessary to ensure that systems are fully recovered and functioning properly. During continuity planning and post-incident recovery, it is important to consider several aspects. First, it is essential to define acceptable recovery times for critical processes and business services. This allows you to establish recovery objectives and allocate the resources necessary to achieve these objectives. Additionally, it is critical to involve all stakeholders, including IT departments, human resources, crisis management and external service providers, to ensure effective collaboration when planning and executing recovery activities. Another aspect to consider is the implementation of testing and evaluation procedures. It is advisable to conduct regular recovery exercises and incident simulations to evaluate the effectiveness of your continuity and recovery plans and identify any weaknesses. These tests allow you to make continuous improvements to incident management strategies and refine procedures to better prepare for future emergencies. Another key aspect in post-incident continuity and recovery planning is the assignment of clear and defined responsibilities at the organizational level. It is important to designate an incident response team composed of members with specific expertise in cybersecurity, emergency management and business recovery. This team should be adequately trained and trained to effectively manage security incidents and coordinate recovery activities. Furthermore, when planning post-incident continuity and recovery, it is crucial to take legal and regulatory aspects into consideration. Organizations should be aware of the laws and regulations applicable to dealing with data security breaches, such as data protection regulations. It is important to understand your legal responsibilities and take appropriate steps to comply with regulatory requirements regarding incident notification, information management and data privacy. In parallel with planning, it is essential to establish an accurate and complete documentation process of all security incident-related events. This includes detailed recording of all activities performed during incident response, decisions made, actions taken and results achieved. Accurate documentation helps you evaluate the effectiveness of your response and recovery strategies, as well as improve procedures for future incidents. Finally, an often overlooked but vitally important aspect is communication during the incident response and recovery process. It is crucial to establish a clear and timely communication plan, both internally and externally, to inform all stakeholders of incident developments, measures taken and recovery progress. This helps maintain the trust of users, customers and other stakeholders, as well as mitigate any reputational damage. In conclusion, post-incident continuity and recovery planning is a complex but vital process to ensure operational resilience and business recovery following a security incident. By identifying critical processes, allocating resources, establishing detailed plans and procedures, implementing tests and evaluations, assigning clear responsibilities, and communicating effectively, organizations can mitigate the negative effects of incidents and restore the security of data and systems in the shortest time possible. Post-incident continuity and recovery planning represents an opportunity to improve incident management capabilities and ensure greater preparedness for future cyber threats.

Role of policies and procedures in safety management

Policies and procedures play a critical role in managing data and information security within an organization. They provide clear guidelines and directives on the security measures to be taken, establishing the rules and expectations for employees and users of the system. Security policies are formal documents that define the organization's security objectives, responsibilities, and procedures. These policies establish the foundation for data protection, resource access, password management, information confidentiality and other essential security practices. Security policies must be regularly reviewed and updated to respond to new threats and technological developments. Security procedures, on the other hand, are operational documents that detail how to implement security policies. These procedures outline the specific actions that must be taken to ensure the security of your data and systems. For example, they may include instructions on how to manage access permissions, how to manage security patches, how to conduct penetration tests, or how to handle security incidents. Security procedures are a practical tool for translating security policies into concrete actions. Correct implementation of security policies and procedures requires commitment at all levels of the organization. It is important that employees and users of the system are aware of the corresponding security policies and procedures. This can be achieved through safety training and awareness programs, which provide employees with the knowledge and skills needed to adopt safe behaviors in their daily work. Additionally, security policies and procedures must be integrated into the organization's operational processes. This means that security must be considered from the beginning in system design and development, project management processes and service delivery. In this way, security becomes an intrinsic aspect of business activities, ensuring consistent and continuous protection of sensitive data and information. Security policies and procedures should be subject to regular review to ensure they are aligned with new threats, regulations and industry best practices. A periodic evaluation process is necessary to identify any gaps or areas for improvement in existing policies and procedures. This can be accomplished through internal or external audits, compliance assessments, penetration testing and other control activities. Finally, it is important to highlight that security policies and procedures are not just static documents, but must be considered dynamic tools. Security management is a continuous and evolving process, where policies and procedures must be constantly updated and adapted to meet new challenges and emerging technologies. Policies and procedures are the foundation on which a robust cybersecurity program is built. In addition to providing guidelines and directives, they play a key role in ensuring compliance with industry regulations and protecting your organization from potential breaches and losses of sensitive data. Security policies establish the fundamental principles that guide the protection of data and information. These policies should be clear, concise and easily understandable for everyone in the organization. They must define the responsibilities of employees and users, establish the rules for access and use of the systems, as well as identify the security measures to be taken to protect information resources. An important aspect of security policies is the management of access permissions. These policies must define who has the right to access certain data and systems and how. They must also establish password management procedures, such as using strong passwords, periodically changing passwords, and limiting access to data only to those who actually need it to perform their jobs. Security procedures, on the other hand, detail the specific actions that must be followed to implement security policies. These procedures can cover different aspects, such as user account management, data protection, vulnerability management, security incident response, and so on. It is important that procedures are easily accessible, with clear instructions and well-defined steps to carry out tasks safely and effectively. Another key component of policies and procedures is security awareness. Policies must be communicated effectively to all employees and users of the organization through security training and awareness programs. These programs educate users about common threats, best security practices, and proper handling of sensitive data. They also promote a security culture in which everyone in the organization feels responsible and involved in protecting information assets. It is critical that policies and procedures are dynamic and subject to constant review. Cyber threats are constantly evolving and policies need to be updated to meet new challenges. It is advisable to regularly conduct internal or external audits to evaluate the effectiveness of policies and procedures and identify any weaknesses. Furthermore, periodic reviews allow policies to be adapted to new technologies and organizational changes. In conclusion, policies and procedures play a vital role in managing cybersecurity. They provide a regulatory and operational framework to ensure data and information protection. Through clear policies, detailed procedures, security awareness, and regular reviews, an organization can mitigate risks, prevent security breaches, and foster a security culture where data protection is a priority for everyone in the organization.

PHYSICAL AND ENVIRONMENTAL SAFETY
Security of premises and data centers

Physical and environmental security is a critical aspect of overall cybersecurity management. It is important to protect not only digital data and information, but also the physical environments in which those assets are hosted. This chapter will explore the key elements of premises and data center security. Premises security is about protecting the physical spaces where computer systems and network resources are located. It is essential to ensure that these spaces are accessible only to authorized personnel and that they are protected from physical intrusion. This can be achieved through a combination of security measures, including access controls, activity monitoring, security cameras, intruder alarms and fire detection systems. Access controls play a crucial role in the security of premises. Procedures must be implemented for the assignment of access badges, for verifying the identity of visitors and for monitoring entries and exits. Additionally, electronic locking systems, such as combination locks or fingerprint readers, can be used to ensure that only authorized personnel have access to the premises. Monitoring activities within the premises is equally important. This can be achieved through the use of strategically placed security cameras, which allow continuous recording and surveillance of spaces. Camera data must be stored securely and protected from unauthorized access. In addition to the security of the premises, it is essential to protect the data centers, which host critical IT systems. Data centers must be designed and built with high standards of physical security, which include elements such as access control systems, fire protection, intrusion detection and critical infrastructure redundancy. Access control systems in data centers must be stringent, limiting access to authorized personnel only. This can be achieved through measures such as using access badges with specific permissions, multi-factor authentication and logging of access activities. Fire protection is critical to preventing damage to data center systems and infrastructure. Fire detection and alarm systems must be installed, together with fire suppression systems such as sprinklers or inert gases. Furthermore, data centers must be designed to minimize the risk of fire, for example by avoiding the accumulation of flammable materials and ensuring proper ventilation. Intrusion detection is another critical component of data center security. This can be achieved through the use of advanced security systems, such as motion sensors, surveillance cameras and intruder alarms. Such systems can detect suspicious activity and alert security personnel to intrusions. The availability of backup electrical power is essential to avoid service interruptions in the event of blackouts or failures of the main electricity network. Data centers are equipped with uninterruptible power supplies (UPS) that provide immediate backup power in the event of a power outage. These UPSs are able to keep critical systems running for a certain period of time, allowing for switching to emergency generators if the outage is prolonged. Emergency generators ensure long-term power supply until the main power supply is restored. Redundant cooling systems are equally important to prevent components from overheating and compromising server performance. Data centers use cooling solutions that include air conditioning units, water refrigeration systems or free-cooling solutions. Redundancy in this context implies the presence of two or more cooling systems, so that if one were to fail or require maintenance, the other can continue to maintain optimal temperatures within the premises. Redundant network connectivity is another crucial aspect to ensure the operational continuity of data centers. This involves using multiple Internet Service Providers and multiple physical connections to ensure continuous availability of your network connection. In the event of a provider or connection failure or interruption, redundant network routes ensure that traffic can be routed via another working connection, avoiding disruptions to services hosted in the data center. Critical infrastructure redundancy requires adequate planning and implementation, with attention to technical details and supplier selection. It is important to ensure that redundant systems are tested regularly for functionality and effectiveness. Additionally, processes and procedures must be documented and communicated to all personnel involved in managing the data center. Maintaining robust redundancy of critical infrastructure is a significant investment, but essential to avoid costly outages and mitigate data security and availability risks. In the event of failure or emergency situations, infrastructure redundancy ensures that the data center can continue to operate reliably, guaranteeing the continuity of services offered to customers and minimizing negative impacts on company activities. In addition to the redundancy of critical infrastructures, the physical and environmental security of premises and data centers is another fundamental aspect to consider in security management. Physical security refers to the measures taken to protect the premises, equipment and data within the data center from unauthorized access, theft, damage or accidents. One of the most common physical security measures is the implementation of access control systems. These systems may include the use of badges, electronic or biometric keys to limit access to sensitive areas of the data center to authorized personnel only. Furthermore, surveillance cameras can be installed to constantly monitor critical areas and record any suspicious activity. In addition to access control systems, data centers can take additional measures to physically secure the premises. These may include the use of security fences, security doors, high security locks and intruder alarms. Additionally, security procedures such as identity verification, access logging, and monitoring of staff activities within the data center could be implemented. Environmental security is equally important to ensure the proper functioning of data centers. This includes managing temperature and humidity, protecting against fires and floods, as well as preventing risks related to air quality and the possible presence of harmful chemicals. To ensure optimal temperature and humidity, data centers are equipped with advanced air conditioning systems that constantly maintain the required levels. Furthermore, sensors and alarms can be installed to detect any changes and problems in the indoor climate. Fire protection is another important component of environmental safety. Data centers are equipped with fire detection and alarm systems, automatic shutdown units such as fire extinguishers or inert gas systems, and evacuation plans in case of emergencies. Preventing air quality risks and the presence of harmful chemicals can be addressed through designing adequate ventilation, monitoring indoor air, and properly managing the materials used within the data center. Additionally, implementing data backup and recovery procedures is essential to protect sensitive data and ensure operational continuity in the event of a physical or environmental incident. Creating backup copies of critical data and storing it in secure locations separate from the primary data center reduces the risk of data loss or corruption in emergency situations. The physical and environmental security of premises and data centers is crucial to protect data, equipment and business operations from potential threats and incidents. Taking appropriate measures, such as access control systems, fire protection, environmental monitoring and data backup procedures, helps ensure a secure and reliable environment for storing and processing business information. In conclusion, physical and environmental security is a critical aspect of data center management. Implementing appropriate security measures, such as access control, fire protection, indoor climate management and data backup procedures, helps ensure the integrity, availability and confidentiality of company data.

Physical access control

Physical access control is a key component of the physical security of premises and data centers. It consists of the implementation of systems and procedures to limit access to sensitive areas only to authorized personnel and prevent unauthorized intrusions. To ensure adequate physical access control, various security tools and mechanisms can be adopted. One of the most common is the use of badges or electronic keys. These devices allow authorized personnel to access restricted areas through access readers that verify the authenticity of the credentials provided. In some cases, biometric authentication, such as fingerprint or iris scan, may be required to further increase security. In addition to physical access control, other security measures can be implemented to protect sensitive areas. For example, entrance doors can be equipped with high-security locks or electronic locking systems. Furthermore, surveillance cameras can be installed to constantly monitor critical areas and record any suspicious activity. These video surveillance systems can be connected to centralized monitors or can use facial recognition technology to identify people entering sensitive areas. It is important that physical access control is managed appropriately through well-defined policies and procedures. This includes assigning appropriate access levels based on staff roles and responsibilities, as well as accurately recording sign-ins and sign-outs. Additionally, safety protocols should be established for external visits, such as suppliers or customers, to ensure they only have access to authorized areas and under strict supervision. Another crucial aspect of physical access control is credential and password management. It is important to establish procedures for the secure distribution of credentials and ensure that passwords are strong and updated regularly. Using two-factor authentication systems can further strengthen security by requiring a second verification method in addition to login credentials, such as a code sent via SMS or an authenticator application. Staff training and awareness play a vital role in ensuring effective physical access control. It is essential that staff are adequately trained in the organization's security policies and procedures and physical access management. This can be achieved through regular training sessions and security awareness programs. During training, staff should be informed about the risks and consequences of a physical security breach. They must be made aware of possible threats, such as unauthorized access or theft of sensitive information. Furthermore, they should be trained on how to recognize suspicious behavior or potentially harmful activities and how to report such situations to the relevant authorities. The training should also include a clear understanding of the organization's security policies and procedures, including protocols for accessing sensitive areas, proper use of credentials and passwords, and handling of guests and visitors. Staff must be aware of the importance of following these policies and procedures to ensure the physical security of the organization. Additionally, staff should be up-to-date on the latest trends and technologies in the field of physical security. This may include information on new access control systems, advanced authentication techniques, or new emerging threats. Keeping staff informed of these developments helps maintain a high level of security and adapt to changing physical security challenges. It is important that training is an ongoing process and is periodically repeated to ensure that staff maintain a good understanding of security policies and procedures. Training sessions can be integrated into the new employee orientation program and repeated as needed by the organization. In addition to training, there are several activities that can help increase staff awareness of physical safety. One of these activities is the display of information posters in work spaces. Posters may contain key physical security information, such as access procedures, personnel identification requirements, or security measures specific to different environments. These posters can serve as a visual reminder for staff and help maintain safety awareness. Distribution of educational materials is another effective strategy to promote staff awareness of physical safety. These materials may include brochures, guides, or manuals that provide detailed information about your organization's security policies, access protocols, and security measures to follow. Educational materials can be distributed in electronic or paper format and can be made available both proactively and as a reference resource for staff. Security awareness sessions are another form of activity that can engage staff in a more interactive way. These sessions may be organized periodically and may include presentations, simulations of real situations or practical exercises. During these sessions, staff can learn more about physical security procedures, understand associated risks, and gain practical skills for dealing with emergency situations or suspicious behavior. Additionally, these sessions can provide an opportunity for staff to ask questions, share experiences, or suggest improvements to existing policies and procedures. Additionally, it is important to create an organizational culture that promotes the importance of physical safety and encourages staff to report any suspicious behavior or situations. This can be done through clearly communicating reporting policies and assuring staff that reports will be taken seriously and handled appropriately. Furthermore, it is useful to encourage staff to be vigilant and attentive when monitoring physical access, encouraging the reporting of any anomalies or behavior inconsistent with security procedures. In conclusion, in addition to training, staff awareness of physical security can be promoted through a variety of activities, such as displaying information posters, distributing educational materials and organizing security awareness sessions. It is also important to create a culture that values safety and encourages staff to report suspicious behavior or situations. These activities help strengthen the physical security of the organization and actively involve personnel in protecting company assets.

Protection of devices and physical storage media

Protecting physical devices and storage media is a critical aspect of physical security. Devices and storage media contain data that is sensitive and valuable to an organization, and therefore must be adequately protected to prevent unauthorized access or loss of information. One of the key measures for protecting physical storage devices and media is the use of locks and physical security devices. Buildings, rooms or areas where devices and storage media are stored must be equipped with secure locks, such as controlled access locks or electronic access control systems. Additionally, mobile or portable devices, such as laptops or external hard drives, should be protected with security devices, such as locks or security cables, to prevent theft or unauthorized physical access. It is also important to protect devices and physical storage media from catastrophic events, such as fires or floods. This can be done through the adoption of environmental protection measures, such as installing smoke detectors, automatic shutdown or fire alarm systems, and the adoption of flood prevention precautions, such as the installation of sensors of water or the organization of devices in elevated areas. Additionally, it is important to implement policies and procedures for the secure management of physical devices and storage media. These policies and procedures may include labeling and cataloging devices and storage media, recording information about their use, and maintaining regular inventory. Furthermore, it is important to establish procedures for the secure destruction of devices and storage media when they are no longer needed, such as the use of physical destruction tools or the use of specialized data destruction services. Protecting devices and physical storage media also requires staff awareness and education. Staff should be informed about best practices for managing and protecting devices and physical storage media, such as the importance of not leaving devices unattended or sharing confidential information in an insecure manner. Additionally, staff must be trained on how to report any accidents or losses of devices and storage media in a timely manner. Staff awareness and education are crucial to ensuring the protection of devices and physical storage media. It is essential that staff are adequately informed about best practices for handling and protecting such devices in order to prevent potential risks or security breaches. One of the first guidelines staff must understand is the importance of not leaving devices unattended. Mobile devices, such as laptops, smartphones or tablets, must always be under the control of the owner and should not be left unattended in public places or accessible to unauthorized persons. Additionally, staff must be aware of the risk of theft or loss of devices and the consequences that may result, such as the potential disclosure of sensitive data or unauthorized access to company resources. Another important aspect is the correct management of confidential information. Staff must be trained on the importance of not sharing sensitive information in an unsafe manner or with unauthorized persons. This includes awareness of threats such as hacking, phishing or communications eavesdropping, and using secure communications channels, such as corporate networks or encryption services, to share sensitive information. Furthermore, staff must be trained on how to promptly report any accidents or losses of devices and storage media. It is important that staff know who to contact in the event of problems or emergency situations, such as the loss or theft of a device. This allows you to promptly activate incident response procedures and take the necessary measures to protect data and limit potential damage. Staff training can be carried out through different methods. In addition to dedicated training sessions, tools such as information posters, brochures or explanatory videos can be used to communicate best practices and raise awareness among staff about the security of devices and physical storage media. Additionally, it is important to maintain a culture of security within the organization, where device and data protection is considered the responsibility of all employees. In conclusion, staff awareness and education play a vital role in protecting physical devices and storage media. Staff must be informed about best practices for managing and protecting devices, including the risks associated with their use and the actions to take in the event of accidents or losses. Only through solid awareness and adequate training can staff become an active participant in defending the physical security of the organization's devices and storage media.

Waste management and secure data disposal

Waste management and secure data disposal are critical aspects of physical security and protection of sensitive information. When devices or physical storage media reach the end of their useful life, it is important to take appropriate measures to ensure that the data contained within them is not accessible to unauthorized third parties. Proper waste management involves establishing specific procedures for the collection, treatment and disposal of obsolete physical storage devices and media. These procedures must comply with environmental regulations and data privacy laws. It is important that your organization works with reputable waste management service providers who can ensure the safe deletion of data and the correct disposal of devices in accordance with applicable regulations. When it comes to secure data deletion, specific processes and techniques must be in place to ensure that information stored on physical devices is no longer recoverable once the device is retired or returned. Wiping data should include the use of secure erasure methods, such as overwriting data or physically destroying the device, to ensure that all sensitive information is irretrievably deleted. Managing waste and secure data disposal requires adequate planning and the establishment of internal procedures. It is important to establish an inventory of devices and physical storage media, monitor the life cycle of devices, and plan for their retirement and disposal in a timely manner. Furthermore, it is essential to keep accurate records of device and data disposal activities, documenting the processes adopted and the results obtained. Staff training is essential to ensure proper waste management and safe data disposal. It is important that personnel are adequately trained on safety standards and procedures to follow during the device disposal process. This includes understanding the importance of protecting sensitive data even after devices are discarded or returned. During training, staff must be informed about the correct ways to handle obsolete devices and physical storage media containing sensitive data. They must be aware of the risks associated with the loss or unauthorized disclosure of information contained in these devices. They should be trained on how to safely handle devices during transportation and temporary storage, avoiding leaving them unattended or accessible to unauthorized third parties. Furthermore, staff must be made aware of the correct ways to delete data and the need to adopt secure deletion methods. They must understand the importance of using tools and procedures that ensure that data is irremediably erased from devices, avoiding the possibility of recovery by third parties. This may include using specialized software to securely overwrite data or physically destroying devices through trusted methods. Staff training must be an ongoing and periodic process to ensure that all employees are always up to date on waste management and data disposal procedures. This may include regular training sessions, educational materials, quizzes or learning tests to assess staff understanding. Additionally, it is important to encourage staff to report any concerns or breaches of procedures in a timely manner, so they can be addressed promptly and correctly. Staff training must be supported by clear and well-documented policies and procedures. These policies should define the requirements for the management of waste and the disposal of sensitive data, specifying the responsibilities of staff and the security measures to be taken. It is important that these policies are easily accessible and understandable to all staff, so that they can be followed correctly. Clear and well-documented policies and procedures are essential to ensure proper management of waste and the disposal of sensitive data. These policies must precisely define the requirements and guidelines to be followed during the waste management and data disposal process. Policies should establish specific responsibilities of personnel involved in waste management and disposal of sensitive data. This may include identifying designated managers to supervise and coordinate these activities, ensuring that appropriate procedures are followed. Additionally, policies should define security measures to protect sensitive data throughout the process, including requirements for secure device access and permanent data deletion. It is essential that these policies are easily accessible and understandable to all staff. Policies and procedures should be documented clearly and in detail, preferably in an easily referenced format such as a manual or guide. This way, staff can refer to the policies whenever they need to manage waste or delete sensitive data, ensuring they are correctly following established procedures. In addition to documenting policies, it is important to provide specific training and guidance to staff. Training should cover policies and procedures, explaining staff responsibilities and outlining safety measures to be taken. It is also useful to provide practical examples and realistic scenarios to help staff understand the importance of properly managing waste and securely disposing of sensitive data. During training, it is useful to involve staff in practical activities or simulations that put them in real situations. This can help solidify your understanding of policies and procedures, as well as identify any points of confusion or questions that require further clarification. Finally, it is important to monitor and evaluate the effectiveness of policies and procedures by collecting feedback from staff and analyzing the results. This can help identify any gaps or areas for improvement, allowing you to make the necessary changes to ensure optimal waste management and secure disposal of sensitive data. In conclusion, clear and well-documented policies and procedures are essential for proper waste management and disposal of sensitive data. These policies must define the requirements and guidelines to be followed, specifying the responsibilities of the staff and the necessary security measures. It is important that these policies are easily accessible and understandable to all staff, and that they are supported by specific training and guidance. Regularly monitoring and evaluating the effectiveness of policies and procedures is critical to ensuring optimal waste management and secure disposal of sensitive data.

PRIVACY AND REGULATORY COMPLIANCE

Fundamental principles of privacy and protection of personal data

Respect for privacy and regulatory compliance are essential to ensure the protection of personal data. There are fundamental principles that guide the proper management of privacy and personal data, and understanding these principles is essential to creating a safe and trustworthy environment. One of the fundamental principles is the data minimization principle. This principle implies that organizations should only collect and use personal data that is necessary for specific, well-defined purposes. Excessive collection and processing of personal data should be avoided, as it may increase the risk of unauthorized access or misuse. Another important principle is the principle of informed consent. This principle requires that people have the ability to make informed decisions about the collection and use of their personal data. Organizations must obtain explicit consent from individuals before collecting or using their personal data, and must provide clear and understandable information about the purposes of the processing and the rights of data subjects. Transparency is another key component in managing privacy and personal data. Organizations must be transparent about their data management practices, communicating their policies and procedures in a clear and accessible way. People need to be informed about how their personal data is collected, used, stored and shared, enabling them to make informed decisions about their privacy. Data security is a crucial aspect in protecting personal data. Organizations must take appropriate security measures to prevent unauthorized access, disclosure or alteration of personal data. This may include implementing access controls, data encryption, securing networks and systems, as well as training staff in secure data handling. Additionally, organizations must comply with laws and regulations regarding privacy and personal data protection. This may include compliance with regulations such as the General

Data Protection Regulation (GDPR) in the European Union or the California Consumer Privacy Act (CCPA) in the United States. Organizations must be aware of the laws applicable in their geographic and industry context and must take steps to ensure compliance with these regulations. Laws and regulations relating to privacy and personal data protection are essential to ensure the protection of individuals' rights and establish a clear regulatory framework for organisations. In order to maintain compliance with these regulations, organizations must adopt a number of measures and procedures. Firstly, it is important that organizations are aware of the laws applicable in their geographical and sectoral context. The General Data Protection Regulation (GDPR) in the European Union is one of the main international privacy references, but there are also other specific regulations in different countries and regions. Organizations must be up to date on relevant regulatory provisions and understand the specific requirements that must be met. Once applicable laws have been identified, organizations must take concrete actions to ensure compliance. This may include the appointment of a data protection officer (DPO) or privacy professional, who has responsibility for monitoring and managing regulatory compliance. These figures can help develop internal policies and procedures, provide advice on the management of personal data and play a key role in communicating with supervisory authorities. Organizations must take technical and organizational measures to protect personal data. This may include implementing appropriate security procedures and technology controls to prevent unauthorized access, disclosure or modification of data. Data encryption, the adoption of network and system security measures, as well as the management of access and authorizations are just some of the aspects to consider to ensure adequate protection of personal data. Additionally, organizations must have policies and procedures in place to handle requests from individuals regarding their personal data. For example, the GDPR provides the right to access, the right to rectification and the right to be forgotten. Organizations must be prepared to respond to these requests in a timely and efficient manner, ensuring that the rights of data subjects are respected. Compliance with privacy regulations also requires an ongoing commitment to evaluating and updating policies and procedures.

Organizations must regularly conduct internal audits to evaluate the effectiveness of the measures taken and make any improvements. Furthermore, they must keep up to date on new regulatory provisions or legislative changes that may affect the management of personal data and adapt their practices accordingly. Periodically evaluating and updating policies and procedures is crucial to ensuring ongoing compliance with privacy regulations. Organizations must conduct regular internal audits to evaluate the effectiveness of the measures taken and identify any gaps or areas for improvement. During the internal audit, it is important to verify whether policies and procedures are aligned with current regulatory provisions. You should carefully review the technical and organizational measures taken to protect personal data, ensuring that they are adequate and sufficient. The audit should also include an assessment of the handling of individuals' requests, verifying that procedures for responding to requests for access, rectification or deletion are correctly implemented. Based on the audit results, organizations should make any improvements to their policies and procedures. This could mean introducing new security measures, updating existing policies or reviewing personal data management processes. It is important to consider feedback from the audit and industry best practices to take a proactive approach to protecting personal data. Furthermore, organizations must constantly keep up to date on new regulatory provisions or legislative changes that could affect the management of personal data. Privacy regulations are constantly evolving and may vary from country to country. It is essential to carefully monitor regulatory developments and adapt policies and procedures accordingly. A good practice is to designate a privacy officer or team dedicated to managing regulatory compliance issues. This figure or team should be responsible for monitoring new regulations, participating in conferences and training on privacy issues and maintaining constant internal updates on the evolution of the regulatory framework. In conclusion, compliance with privacy regulations requires an ongoing commitment to evaluating and updating policies and procedures. Internal audits, review of security measures, adaptation to new regulatory provisions and the designation of a privacy officer are all fundamental elements to maintain effective and compliant management of personal data. Only through a diligent and ongoing approach to regulatory compliance can organizations adequately protect personal data and maintain the trust of users and customers.

Privacy legislation and regulations

Privacy legislation and regulations are legal instruments that aim to protect people's rights and privacy by regulating the collection, use, storage and disclosure of personal data. These laws have been introduced at international, national and regional levels to address growing concerns about data privacy and security. Internationally, one of the most influential regulations is the European Union's General Data Protection Regulation (GDPR). The GDPR came into force in 2018 and establishes a comprehensive regulatory framework for the protection of personal data of EU citizens. It requires organizations to respect fundamental principles such as transparency in data collection, informed consent, purpose limitation, data minimization and data security. The GDPR also introduced broader individual rights, such as the right to access, rectification, erasure and data portability. In the United States, there are different privacy laws at the federal and state levels. One of the most significant is the California Consumer Privacy Act (CCPA), which went into effect in 2020. The CCPA gives California consumers the right to know what personal data organizations collect and share, the right to request deletion of their data, and the right to object to the sale of your personal data. Other state laws, such as the New York Privacy Act (NYPA) and the Virginia Consumer Data Protection Act (VCDPA), have been introduced to broaden personal data protections and give users more rights and control over their privacy. Beyond these specific regulations, many countries and regions have developed privacy laws that are inspired by the fundamental principles outlined in regulations such as the GDPR. These laws define the rights and responsibilities of organizations and individuals regarding the protection of personal data. Privacy laws often require organizations to take technical and organizational measures to protect personal data, to inform users about their data collection and use practices, and to obtain explicit consent from users when required. Privacy laws and regulations are continually evolving to address emerging challenges related to privacy and data security. It is important for organizations to carefully monitor legislative changes in their geographic and sectoral context and adapt their practices to maintain regulatory compliance. Violating privacy regulations can result in serious consequences, including significant fines and damage to your organization's reputation. Therefore, it is essential that organizations understand and comply with privacy laws and regulations to ensure adequate protection of personal data and maintain the trust of their users and customers. Furthermore, privacy laws and regulations can vary greatly from one country to another. For example, some countries may have more stringent data protection and user consent laws, while others may have less stringent regulations. Therefore, organizations operating internationally must be aware of different regulations and adapt accordingly to ensure compliance across all affected jurisdictions. Compliance with privacy laws and regulations requires ongoing efforts from organizations. It is essential to establish internal policies and procedures that reflect the fundamental principles of privacy and protection of personal data. These policies should clearly define how personal data is collected, used, stored and disclosed, as well as the security measures taken to protect it. Furthermore, processes should be established to handle user requests regarding their personal data, such as access, rectification or deletion. Organizations must also appoint a privacy officer or data protection officer (DPO) who has in-depth knowledge of privacy laws and regulations and is responsible for ensuring compliance within the organisation. The DPO will work with internal departments to implement privacy policies and procedures, conduct internal audits to assess compliance, and provide training and consultation to staff. Furthermore, it is important to highlight that regulatory compliance is not only about the legal aspect, but also about the ethical responsibility of organizations. Organizations must demonstrate a commitment to privacy and the protection of personal data, going beyond compliance with basic standards. This may include adopting advanced security measures, implementing appropriate data retention policies and adopting transparent practices that put users at the center of decisions about the management of personal data. Finally, organizations must maintain a mindset of continuous learning and adaptation to new challenges and changes in the field of privacy and personal data protection. They must stay up to date on new laws and regulations that may affect the handling of personal data and make necessary changes to their policies and procedures accordingly. Compliance with privacy laws and regulations not only helps protect individuals' rights and prevent privacy violations, but also helps build a strong reputation and trust in the organization. Through responsible and conscious management of personal data, organizations can establish lasting relationships of trust with their users and customers, promoting privacy as a fundamental value in today's digital society. In conclusion, compliance with privacy laws and regulations is imperative for any organization that handles personal data. These laws were introduced to protect the rights of individuals and ensure that their data is treated securely and responsibly. In addition to complying with legal regulations, regulatory compliance promotes user and customer trust, contributing to a positive reputation for the organization. To achieve compliance, organizations must develop robust policies and procedures that reflect the fundamental principles of privacy and personal data protection. These policies must be implemented effectively, involving all staff and ensuring they are easily accessible and understandable. Staff training is essential to ensure compliance with privacy regulations. Staff must be aware of their duties and responsibilities when processing personal data and must be trained on the correct procedures to follow. Additionally, employees must be informed about users' rights regarding their personal data and how to handle user requests in a timely and effective manner. It is also important to highlight that compliance with privacy regulations is not a static goal, but requires an ongoing commitment from the organization. Privacy laws and regulations may evolve over time, so organizations must stay up to date on new regulatory requirements and adapt their policies and procedures accordingly. Finally, compliance with privacy laws is not only a legal obligation, but also an ethical commitment. Organizations must demonstrate their commitment to protecting personal data by adopting advanced security measures, promoting transparency and informed user consent, and managing data responsibly. Compliance with privacy laws and regulations requires a collective effort across the organization. Only through a well-entrenched privacy culture and responsible management of personal data can organizations protect users' interests and build lasting relationships of trust with their customers.

Best practices for managing personal data

Managing personal data requires the adoption of best practices that enable organizations to ensure the safe, responsible and ethical processing of individuals' personal data. These best practices are based on fundamental principles of privacy and data protection, which aim to promote transparency, security and respect for privacy. An important best practice is informed consent. Organizations must obtain explicit and informed consent from users before collecting, using or sharing their personal data. Consent must be voluntary and based on clear and understandable information. It is vital that organizations provide users with a clear understanding of how their personal data will be used and for what purposes. Another crucial aspect is the limitation of data collection. Organizations must only collect personal data that is strictly necessary for specific and legitimate purposes. It is important to avoid excessive or unnecessary data collection. This involves careful evaluation of the information that needs to be collected and careful design of data collection forms and processes. Data security is another key best practice. Organizations must implement appropriate security measures to protect personal data from unauthorized access, loss, alteration or improper disclosure. This may include using encryption tools to protect data during transmission and storage, implementing access controls to limit access to data to authorized personnel only, and implementing backup and data recovery to ensure data availability and integrity. An important aspect of personal data management is limited data retention. Organizations must retain personal data only for as long as strictly necessary to achieve the purposes for which it was collected. You must establish appropriate retention periods and implement procedures to delete or anonymize data at the end of the retention period. This avoids prolonged storage of personal data without legitimate justification. Transparency and user rights are essential aspects of personal data management. Organizations must inform users clearly and completely about their rights regarding their personal data. These rights include the right to access, the right to rectification, the right to be forgotten and the right to withdraw consent. It is important that organizations provide simple and effective ways for users to exercise these rights. Furthermore, organizations must be transparent about their data management practices, providing users with detailed information on the purposes of data collection, how it is processed and whether it is shared with third parties. Another best practice is privacy impact assessment. Organizations must conduct privacy impact assessments to identify and mitigate risks associated with personal data processing activities. This assessment may include analyzing the purposes of the processing, assessing the risks to the privacy of the affected individuals and identifying measures to mitigate those risks. Furthermore, it is advisable to implement the principle of privacy by design, which involves integrating privacy considerations from the initial stages of product or service development. Finally, organizations must continually monitor their personal data practices and conduct periodic reviews to ensure compliance with privacy best practices and regulations. It is important to stay up to date on new regulatory provisions or legislative changes that may affect the management of personal data and to make any changes or improvements to your data management policies and procedures. Adopting these best practices for managing personal data helps organizations ensure responsible and respectful processing of individuals' personal data, promoting trust and transparency in relationships with users. Furthermore, adopting these best practices for managing personal data brings numerous benefits to organizations themselves. First, it helps you avoid potential breaches of privacy and data protection regulations, thereby reducing the risk of legal and reputational sanctions. Regulatory compliance is an increasingly important requirement, especially given the increase in privacy regulations around the world. Second, implementing these best practices helps build and maintain a positive reputation for the organization. When users feel safe and confident in the way their personal data is handled, they are more likely to maintain a long-term relationship with the organization by providing their data and using its products or services. Trust and transparency in the management of personal data can be real competitive advantages for an organization in today's market. Furthermore, correct management of personal data promotes the quality of the data itself.

Maintaining accurate and constant control over personal data will allow organizations to have accurate and up-to-date information on their users, which can be used for marketing purposes, market analysis or the development of personalized products and services. Data quality can directly impact an organization's ability to make effective strategic decisions. Finally, responsible management of personal data demonstrates the organization's commitment to protecting the privacy and rights of individuals. This can help create a privacy-oriented company culture, where employees are aware of the importance of processing personal data ethically and securely. Promoting a culture of privacy can be an added value for the organization, both internally and externally. Promoting a privacy-oriented corporate culture is a key aspect of ensuring responsible management of personal data. This involves involving all levels of the organization, from rank-and-file staff to management, in adopting practices and behaviors that respect individuals' privacy. A privacy-oriented corporate culture starts with staff awareness and training. Employees must be informed about the fundamental principles of privacy and applicable legislation, such as the GDPR or other personal data protection laws. They must understand the importance of protecting personal data, both during its collection and during its use and storage. Training must be ongoing and tailored to the specific needs of the organization, taking into account regulatory changes and new threats or challenges related to data privacy. In addition to training, you need to promote a culture of privacy through well-documented policies and procedures. These policies should establish employees' responsibilities in handling personal data, define the security measures to be taken and establish the consequences for any breaches of privacy. It is important that these policies are easily accessible to all employees and that they are regularly updated to respond to regulatory changes or new privacy challenges. Additionally, creating a culture of privacy requires committed leadership and example from executives. Leaders must demonstrate an ongoing commitment to protecting the privacy and rights of individuals, both through words and actions. They must promote the importance of privacy within the organization and ensure that the necessary resources are allocated to ensure the safety and protection of personal data. Executive commitment helps foster a privacy mindset among employees and creates an environment where data protection is considered a priority. Finally, promoting a culture of privacy can provide added value both internally and externally. Internally, it creates a work environment where employees feel safer and more protected, knowing that their privacy is respected. This can improve efficiency and productivity, as employees focus on their work without concerns about the security of personal data. Externally, a culture of privacy can be a differentiator for the organization. Users and customers will be more inclined to choose an organization that demonstrates a serious commitment to privacy and personal data protection. Finally, fostering a culture of privacy within an organization offers numerous internal and external benefits. Internally, a culture of privacy creates a work environment where employees feel safer and more secure about the management of their personal data. This, in turn, can have a positive impact on employee efficiency and productivity. When employees know that their privacy is respected and that personal data is handled appropriately, they can better focus on work tasks without worrying about unintended consequences or security risks. This can foster greater trust between staff and the organization, creating a positive and collaborative working climate. Furthermore, a culture of privacy can help improve the organization's reputation and increase the trust of customers and external users. In an era where privacy concerns are increasingly widespread, people are increasingly careful about how their personal information is handled by the organizations they interact with. An organization that demonstrates a serious commitment to privacy and the protection of personal data will be seen as more trustworthy and respectful of people's rights. This positive reputation can translate into a competitive advantage for the organization, as customers and users will be more inclined to choose an organization that ensures responsible and secure processing of their personal data. The trust gained can also foster long-term relationships with customers, promoting customer retention and loyalty. Additionally, a culture of privacy can help mitigate the legal and financial risks associated with privacy violations and improper handling of personal data. By taking appropriate security measures and complying with privacy laws and regulations, an organization reduces the likelihood of incurring penalties, fines or legal action that could result from privacy violations. In conclusion, promoting a privacy-oriented corporate culture offers numerous internal and external benefits. Internally, it creates a work environment where employees feel safe and secure, improving efficiency and productivity. Externally, it helps improve the organization's reputation and attract the trust of customers and users. In an increasingly stringent regulatory environment and in an era where privacy is a growing concern, a culture of privacy can be a differentiator and add value for any organization.

Compliance with industry regulations and standards

Compliance with regulations and industry standards is an essential aspect of effectively managing data security and privacy. Organizations must be aware of the relevant laws and regulations in their sector and jurisdiction, as well as internationally recognized standards and guidelines. Regulations and industry standards are developed to ensure the protection of personal data, promote transparency and accountability of organizations, as well as provide clear guidelines on the management of sensitive data. Some of the most relevant regulations include the General Data Protection Regulation (GDPR) in the European Union, the California Consumer Privacy Act (CCPA) in the United States, and many other privacy laws in different countries. Compliance with these regulations implies compliance with legislative provisions, including the collection, processing, storage and transmission of personal data. Organizations must establish internal policies and procedures to ensure that personal data is handled in accordance with applicable regulations. This may include the designation of a data protection officer (DPO) or privacy officer, who is responsible for implementing and monitoring data protection policies. Additionally, organizations must regularly evaluate the effectiveness of their security measures and conduct internal audits to verify regulatory compliance. It is important to maintain accurate documentation of the policies and procedures implemented, as well as the results of audits and corrective actions taken. In addition to regulations, industry standards provide specific guidelines for personal data management and information security. For example, the ISO/IEC 27001:2013 standard provides a framework for implementing an information security management system (ISMS), which may include the management of personal data. Compliance with industry standards is often assessed through external audits conducted by independent certification bodies. Obtaining a compliance certification can demonstrate to external stakeholders that your organization adheres to best data management and security practices. Finally, maintaining compliance with regulations and industry standards requires ongoing commitment. Organizations need to stay up to date on new laws and regulations that may be introduced and adapt their policies and procedures accordingly. Furthermore, they must monitor technological developments and new security threats to ensure that protection measures are always adequate and up to date. Compliance with regulations and industry standards is critical to protecting individuals' privacy and personal data. It helps create an environment of trust and ensures that organizations take appropriate measures to prevent privacy breaches and protect sensitive data. Maintaining compliance with regulations and industry standards is not only a legal obligation, but also offers numerous benefits to organizations. First, it demonstrates the organization's commitment to the security and privacy of personal data, increasing the trust of users, customers and business partners. This trust can lead to a better reputation of the organization in the market and greater customer loyalty. Additionally, compliance with regulations and industry standards can reduce the risk of data breaches and resulting penalties and fines. Privacy regulations, such as the GDPR, provide severe penalties for organizations that do not comply with data protection provisions. Being compliant with regulations reduces the risk of lawsuits and reputational damage that could result from a data breach. Additionally, regulatory compliance can enable organizations to access new markets. Some countries or industries require you to comply with certain privacy regulations in order to operate or engage in certain activities. Being compliant with these regulations can open up new business opportunities and allow your organization to expand into new markets. Compliance with regulations and industry standards also helps foster a company culture focused on security and privacy. When organizations adopt policies and procedures to ensure compliance, it creates a mindset of shared responsibility within the organization. Employees become more aware of data security and the implications of privacy violations, contributing to more careful and responsible management of personal information. Finally, compliance with regulations and industry standards can provide a competitive advantage to your organization. In the digital age, the protection of personal data has become an increasingly important concern for individuals and organizations. Users and customers are more likely to trust and prefer organizations that demonstrate a serious commitment to privacy and data protection. Being compliant with industry regulations and standards can therefore position the organization advantageously over competitors. Indeed, in the digital age we find ourselves in, the protection of personal data has become a priority concern for individuals and organizations. The spread of digital technologies and the increasingly massive collection of data have raised numerous concerns about the privacy and security of personal information. Users and customers have become more aware of the risks associated with unauthorized disclosure or misuse of their personal data, and as a result, they have begun to pay more attention to responsible management of the information they share with organizations. Being compliant with regulations and industry standards regarding the protection of personal data can represent a significant competitive advantage for an organization. Users and customers are likely to choose service providers or products that demonstrate a serious commitment to privacy and data protection. The organization's reputation and the trust it inspires can have a significant impact on users' decisions to share their personal information or do business with the organization. Complying with industry regulations and standards requires a holistic approach to managing personal data. This involves adopting well-defined policies and procedures for collecting, processing, storing and sharing personal data, as well as managing user requests regarding the privacy of their data. It also means putting in place technical and organizational measures to protect personal data from unauthorized access, loss or improper disclosure. Compliance with industry regulations and standards requires constant monitoring and careful evaluation of your organization's policies and practices. Privacy laws and regulations are constantly evolving and require constant updating of business practices to maintain compliance with new provisions. Additionally, industry standards and best practices can provide useful guidelines to continuously improve the management of personal data and adapt to new threats and technologies. Ultimately, being compliant with regulations and industry standards can lead to greater user and customer trust. When an organization demonstrates a serious commitment to protecting personal data and respects the privacy of individuals, it creates an environment of trust and transparency that fosters long-term relationships. User trust can translate into greater loyalty, an increase in referrals and a better positioning of the organization in the market. In conclusion, compliance with regulations and industry standards regarding personal data protection can provide a competitive advantage to your organization. Being in line with regulations and adopting best practices for managing personal data builds trust, promotes the organization's reputation and encourages choice among users and customers. Investing in personal data protection is not only a legal obligation, but it can also be a differentiator that contributes to your organization's long-term success in today's digital landscape.

MOBILE SECURITY AND BYOD
Mobile device and app security

Mobile security and the BYOD (Bring Your Own Device) phenomenon represent significant challenges for organizations in terms of data protection and security management. With the increased use of mobile devices such as smartphones and tablets for work purposes, it is critical that adequate security measures are in place to protect both the mobile devices themselves and the sensitive business information they access. Mobile device security starts with implementing clear policies and procedures. Organizations should establish guidelines on the types of mobile devices allowed to access company data and define the security requirements that must be met. This may include using strong passwords, enabling data encryption, installing security software, and managing app permissions. A critical aspect of mobile security is app protection. Organizations should promote the use of apps that are secure, have been evaluated for trustworthiness, and offer data protection features. It's important to educate staff on best practices for installing and using apps, such as avoiding downloading apps from untrusted sources and regularly updating apps to patch any security vulnerabilities. In addition to policies and procedures, mobile security also requires appropriate technological solutions. Organizations should consider implementing mobile device management (MDM) solutions that allow them to centrally monitor and manage mobile devices used within the organization. These solutions help you enforce security policies, configure devices, apply software updates, and manage access to company data. Staff training and awareness are essential to ensure proper management of mobile security and BYOD. Staff must be aware of the risks associated with the use of mobile devices and the importance of following established security policies and procedures. They need to be informed about potential threats, such as phishing or device theft, and how to prevent such situations. To ensure proper management of mobile security and BYOD, staff training and awareness are essential. Staff must be adequately informed about the risks associated with the use of mobile devices and the need to follow the security policies and procedures established by the organization. The training should cover a range of topics, including potential threats that can affect mobile devices, such as phishing, malware, and theft or physical loss of devices. Staff should be trained on how to recognize and manage these threats, adopting good security practices such as using strong passwords, installing apps only from trusted sources, and regularly updating software and apps. Additionally, staff should be aware of the security policies and procedures established by the organization. This includes the importance of protecting sensitive company data and not sharing confidential information insecurely. They must be educated on how to use mobile devices securely and how to properly manage access to company data, using tools such as virtual private networks (VPNs) when accessing sensitive information from public networks. Staff awareness can be promoted through various activities. In addition to initial training, it is advisable to organize periodic refresher sessions to keep staff informed of new threats and security best practices. Additionally, displaying informative posters, distributing educational materials and sharing case studies can help raise awareness of mobile safety and promote responsible behavior. Another important aspect is to encourage staff to report any suspicious behavior or situations related to mobile security. They must feel comfortable reporting security incidents, such as receiving phishing messages or losing a device, so that response measures can be activated promptly. Finally, mobile security and BYOD require a collaborative approach between the organization and its staff. Actively involving employees in defining security policies and implementing security measures can have numerous benefits. First, involving employees in defining security policies allows you to obtain a diverse point of view and consider the needs and perspectives of all stakeholders. This participatory process promotes a sense of ownership and shared responsibility towards the security of corporate information. Employees will be more likely to adhere to safety policies if they feel involved in the decision-making process. Additionally, encouraging employees to provide feedback and suggestions to improve existing security measures creates an environment that promotes innovation and the sharing of best practices. Employees can gain valuable insight into possible vulnerabilities or suggest more efficient solutions to ensure the security of mobile devices and apps used. This helps maintain a dynamic and evolving approach to mobile security. Involving staff in defining safety policies and implementing safety measures also fosters a greater sense of responsibility. Employees will realize the importance of their individual action in maintaining the security of company data and will feel responsible for protecting sensitive information. This can lead to more conscious and attentive behavior when using mobile devices and accessing company data. Finally, involving employees in the mobile security process creates an environment of trust and collaboration. Employees will feel listened to and have greater trust in the organization, knowing that their concerns and contributions are taken into account. This, in turn, can improve company culture, promote transparency and strengthen bonds between the organization and its staff. Furthermore, to ensure proper management of mobile security and BYOD, it is essential to provide ongoing training and awareness to staff. The training should cover several aspects, such as awareness of the risks associated with the use of mobile devices, best practices for device and app security, and the security policies and procedures established by the organization. Training should be targeted and personalized to meet the specific needs of your staff. It may be useful to organize interactive training sessions, using practical examples and realistic scenarios to illustrate potential risks and countermeasures to be taken. It is important that staff understand the implications of their actions and know how to protect sensitive data when using mobile devices. Raising awareness must go beyond initial training and must be an ongoing process. Threats and attack techniques are constantly evolving, so staff must be informed of the latest developments and new security measures. This may include sending periodic security alerts, sharing relevant information through internal channels, such as newsletters or intranets, and organizing periodic update sessions. It is important to actively involve staff in mobile security and BYOD. This can be done by encouraging the reporting of incidents or suspicious behaviour, providing an open and safe communication channel for reports. Additionally, it is helpful to involve employees in reviewing and updating security policies and procedures, allowing them to provide feedback and suggestions. Finally, it is critical that your organization provides adequate resources for mobile security and BYOD. This can include adopting mobile device management (MDM) tools that allow you to apply security policies, monitor and manage devices centrally. Furthermore, the organization should consider using safe and certified apps for mobile working, avoiding the installation of untrusted or unverified apps. In conclusion, staff training and awareness are essential to ensure correct management of mobile security and BYOD. Actively involving staff, providing personalized training, promoting incident reporting and providing adequate resources are key elements to creating a safe environment where staff understand and adhere to established safety policies. Only through a holistic and collaborative approach will it be possible to effectively protect data and mitigate the risks associated with the use of mobile devices and apps.

BYOD policies and best practices for secure use of personal devices in the workplace

Bring Your Own Device (BYOD) policies and best practices for the safe use of personal devices in the workplace are crucial to ensuring the security of company data and protecting your organization from potential threats. Allowing employees to use their own personal devices can improve productivity and flexibility, but requires a strategic approach to minimize the associated risks. The first important consideration is implementing a clear and well-defined BYOD policy. This policy should establish guidelines for the use of personal devices, defining the responsibilities of the employee and the organization, as well as the security measures to be followed. The policy should include requirements such as installing security software, using strong passwords, enabling encryption features, and only accessing secure networks. Another important aspect is the use of mobile device management (MDM) tools to apply and enforce security policies. These tools allow your organization to centrally manage employee devices, enforce security policies, update software, and monitor device usage. Your organization can use MDM to ensure that personal devices are properly configured, encrypted, and updated regularly to mitigate security risks. Additionally, it's critical to educate employees on best practices for using personal devices safely in the workplace. This may include the importance of keeping devices updated with the latest security patches, avoiding installing apps that are unverified or from untrusted sources, and being wary of practices connecting to unsecure public Wi-Fi networks. Employees should also be aware of threats such as phishing and adopt safe browsing practices, avoiding clicking on suspicious links or sharing sensitive information via unsafe messages. Likewise, the organization must provide resources and clear guidelines to employees on how to protect company data on personal devices. This could include using secure sync and share applications and services, secure remote access to company data, and acopting data encryption solutions. Protecting corporate data on personal devices requires taking specific security measures. One of the first best practices is to use secure sync and share applications and services. These solutions allow employees to access company data securely, while ensuring data is encrypted during transfer and storage. This protects sensitive data from unauthorized access and possible security breaches. Additionally, secure remote access to company data is critical when using personal devices in the workplace. Remote access tools allow employees to securely connect to company servers and internal systems, ensuring that data is transmitted encrypted and that appropriate authentication controls are applied to verify users' identities. This reduces the risk of unauthorized access to company data and helps preserve their confidentiality and integrity. Finally, adopting data encryption solutions is an important security measure to protect company data on personal devices. Data encryption makes information unintelligible to anyone without the correct decryption key, ensuring that data is protected even if the device is physically accessed. Your organization should promote the use of data encryption tools on employees' personal devices, so that company data is protected both in transit and at storage. It is important to provide employees with clear resources and guidelines on how to properly use these data protection solutions. This may include training and awareness sessions on best practices for using personal devices securely, as well as providing detailed, accessible documentation that explains step-by-step how to properly set up and use encryption applications, services and solutions. Training and raising awareness of employees on the correct use of data protection solutions is essential to ensure safe management of personal devices in the workplace. This can be achieved through dedicated training sessions, which illustrate the best practices for the safe use of personal devices and the procedures to follow to ensure the protection of company data. During these training sessions, it is important to provide concrete examples and real-world situations to illustrate the risks associated with the use of personal devices and how to mitigate them. For example, you might talk about the dangers of phishing and the importance of avoiding clicking on suspicious links or providing sensitive information in unverified messages or emails. Furthermore, the provision of detailed and accessible documentation is essential to allow employees to refer to the guidelines whenever they need them. This documentation should be clear, concise, and easily understandable, providing step-by-step instructions on how to properly configure and use encryption applications, services, and solutions. It should also explain the reasons behind the security measures and the benefits they bring to protecting company data. Additionally, it's important to encourage employees to ask questions, provide feedback, and report any issues or concerns related to the security of their personal devices. This can be done through internal communication channels, such as emails, forums or question and answer sessions. In this way, a collaborative environment is created in which employees feel involved in data protection and an attitude of shared responsibility is promoted. Finally, it is essential to keep these resources and guidelines up to date. Cyber threats evolve rapidly, and as a result data protection solutions must continually be reviewed and improved. The organization should monitor new industry trends and best practices and adapt its policies and procedures accordingly. In summary, providing employees with clear resources and guidelines, along with training and awareness sessions, is critical to ensuring safe use of personal devices in the workplace. This helps protect company data, reduces security risks and promotes a culture of responsibility and awareness in data management.

Managing the risks associated with the use of mobile devices

Managing the risks associated with the use of mobile devices is a key element in ensuring the security of company information. There are several risks that can arise from the use of mobile devices, such as loss or theft of the device, unauthorized access to information, malware infection or interception of communications. To effectively manage these risks, organizations can take several security measures. First, it's important to implement clear and well-defined mobile security policies. These policies should establish rules for the use of mobile devices in the enterprise, such as installing applications only from trusted sources, encrypting data, using strong passwords, and enabling remote location and lock features . Additionally, the organization should consider adopting enterprise mobility management (Mobile Device Management - MDM) solutions. These solutions allow you to centrally control and manage the mobile devices used by employees. Through MDM, you can set security policies, apply patches and software updates, monitor device usage, and even remotely wipe data if your device is lost or stolen. Another important aspect is the implementation of data encryption solutions on mobile devices. Encryption can be used to protect sensitive data stored on devices, preventing unauthorized access in the event of device loss or theft. It is important that employees are aware of the importance of using encryption and correctly configuring security settings on their mobile devices. Managing the risks associated with mobile device use also requires an app management policy. Organizations should establish clear guidelines on installing applications on company devices and promote the use of apps from trusted sources, such as official app stores. Additionally, it's important to educate employees about the risks of malicious or unauthorized apps and how to recognize and avoid them. Finally, it is essential to constantly monitor the mobile device usage environment to promptly identify any anomalies or security breaches. This can be done through recording and analyzing mobile device activity, implementing threat detection systems, and adopting monitoring and reporting policies. To monitor the mobile device usage environment, we recommend using activity logging and analysis tools. These tools allow you to record and track activities performed on mobile devices, such as accessing applications, sending messages or using network resources. Activity logging can be helpful in identifying any suspicious behavior or security breaches. Additionally, it is important to implement threat detection systems on mobile devices. These systems use algorithms and behavior patterns to identify potential threats or anomalous activity that could indicate an attempted security breach. For example, a threat detection system might detect the installation of an unauthorized application or access to sensitive resources by a compromised device. At the same time, it is advisable to adopt monitoring and reporting policies to ensure constant supervision of the use of mobile devices. These policies may include requiring employees to allow remote access to devices for monitoring and security purposes. Through monitoring, you can identify behaviors or activities that could pose a security risk and take immediate steps to mitigate those risks. Reporting is an essential element of mobile device monitoring. Your organization should implement a reporting system that allows you to generate detailed reports on mobile device usage, detected threats, security breaches and other relevant metrics. These reports provide a comprehensive overview of the situation and allow the organization to make informed decisions and implement corrective actions when necessary. It is important to underline that the monitoring of mobile devices must be carried out with respect for employee privacy and in full compliance with laws and regulations regarding the protection of personal data. The organization must ensure that monitoring is proportionate and that appropriate employee consent is obtained where required. It is critical that your organization respects employee privacy when tracking mobile devices. This means that monitoring must be conducted in accordance with personal data protection laws and regulations, such as the General Data Protection Regulation (GDPR) in the European Union or national privacy laws in the United States. Before initiating any monitoring activity, the organization should carefully evaluate the necessity and proportionality of monitoring. It is important that monitoring is justified by legitimate reasons and that appropriate measures are taken to ensure that only what is necessary to achieve safety objectives is carried out. For example, you may need to monitor only certain types of activity or limit monitoring to certain employees with access to sensitive information. Additionally, the organization must obtain appropriate consent from employees, where required, for the monitoring of their mobile devices. Consent should be informed and voluntary, and employees must be adequately informed about the nature and extent of the monitoring, as well as the rights they have in relation to the protection of their personal data. The organization should also implement technical and organizational measures to protect the data collected during monitoring. This may include adopting data encryption measures, limiting access to the information collected and establishing appropriate data retention periods. Finally, it is important that your organization maintains adequate transparency with employees regarding its mobile device tracking policies and practices. Clear and understandable information should be provided on the purposes of the monitoring, how it is implemented and the rights of employees in relation to their privacy. In conclusion, when monitoring mobile devices, it is essential that the organization respects employee privacy by adopting an approach that complies with personal data protection laws and regulations, assessing the necessity and proportionality of monitoring, obtaining employee consent employees, protecting the data collected and ensuring adequate transparency. These elements are fundamental to balancing the security of company information with respect for employee privacy.

CYBERSECURITY LAWS
Cybersecurity legislation in USA

In the United States, cybersecurity legislation has been introduced to address growing cyber threats and attacks that can damage IT systems, compromise data security, and put individuals' privacy at risk. One of the most important laws in this context is the Computer Fraud and Abuse Act (CFAA), which regulates computer crimes and establishes the related sanctions. This act punishes activities such as unauthorized access to computer systems, the spread of computer viruses, theft of personal data, and other forms of cybercrime. The objective of these provisions is deterrent, so as to discourage people from committing cybercrimes and to protect victims from such attacks. Another relevant regulation is the Cybersecurity Information Sharing Act (CISA). This act provides a series of rules and guidelines to promote cybersecurity in public and private organizations. The Cybersecurity Information Sharing Act encourages the sharing of cybersecurity threat information between the government and the private sector. It also provides legal protections for companies that share cyber threat indicators and defensive measures with federal agencies, aiming to improve collective cybersecurity. In addition to these laws, the United States has also adopted specific regulations for particular sectors, such as the financial and healthcare sectors. For example, the Gramm-Leach-Bliley Act (GLBA) establishes regulations on cybersecurity for financial institutions, requiring them to protect consumers' personal financial information. The Health Insurance Portability and Accountability Act (HIPAA) has issued provisions to ensure the security of sensitive patient health information, mandating the implementation of security measures to protect electronic health records (EHRs). The main goal of these cybersecurity laws is to protect individuals' computer systems, personal data, and privacy. Their implementation requires constant commitment from organizations and competent authorities to ensure compliance and address the ever-evolving challenges in the field of cybersecurity. Furthermore, there are other articles and regulations that specifically address issues related to cybersecurity. One of them is the Cybersecurity Act of 2015, which concerns the sharing of cybersecurity threat information and the implementation of cybersecurity best practices. This act encourages organizations to share information about cyber threats with the government to better protect against attacks. Penalties for cybersecurity crimes may include imprisonment and fines. Additionally, individual states in the U.S. have enacted their own cybersecurity laws and regulations. For example, the California Consumer Privacy Act (CCPA) provides California residents with rights over their personal data, including the right to access, delete, and opt out of the sale of personal information. The New York SHIELD Act strengthens data security requirements for businesses to protect sensitive data. It is important to underline that cybersecurity legislation in the United States is constantly evolving to adapt to new emerging threats and challenges in the field of cybersecurity. It is therefore essential that organizations and individuals stay informed about current regulations and best practices for protecting information systems and personal data.

Cybersecurity legislation in Europe

Cybersecurity legislation in Europe has been the subject of development and harmonization to address the ever-increasing challenges in the field of cybersecurity. One of the main regulatory instruments in this area is the General Data Protection Regulation (GDPR), which entered into force in the European Union in May 2018. The GDPR has a significant impact on cybersecurity, as it establishes strict requirements for the protection of personal data and defines the responsibilities of organizations in processing such data. The regulation requires organizations to take appropriate technical and organizational measures to ensure the security of personal data and to notify data breaches to the relevant authorities and affected individuals. In addition to the GDPR, the European Union has also adopted the Network and Information Security Directive (NIS Directive). This directive establishes requirements for the security of critical networks and information systems in key sectors such as energy, transport, healthcare and digital infrastructure. EU Member States are required to implement the NIS Directive into their national legislation, in order to ensure a high level of cyber security throughout the Union. In addition to these regulations, there are also European-level initiatives and bodies working to promote cybersecurity. For example, the European Union Agency for Cyber Security (ENISA) plays an important role in promoting best practices in cybersecurity and providing advice and support to Member States. It is important to note that cybersecurity legislation may vary from country to country within the European Union, as member states have the discretion to adopt additional provisions to address national specificities. Therefore, organizations operating at a European level must be aware of the specific regulations of the countries in which they operate and take appropriate measures to comply with local laws and ensure data security. Another significant initiative at the European level is the proposed European Union Cybersecurity Regulation, which aims to further strengthen cyber security in the EU. This regulation provides for the establishment of a common framework for managing cyber security at European level and defines the responsibilities of the actors involved, including organisations, Member States and competent authorities. The proposed regulation aims to improve cooperation between Member States in addressing cross-border cyber threats, ensure the security of critical infrastructure and promote the adoption of advanced security measures. Furthermore, it introduces the obligation for organizations to report cybersecurity incidents to the relevant authorities. In addition to specific regulations on cybersecurity, there are also other initiatives at European level aimed at promoting collaboration and information exchange between Member States. For example, the European Union Agency for Law Enforcement Cooperation (Europol) plays an important role in the fight against cybercrime at the European level, facilitating cooperation between law enforcement agencies and providing investigative and operational support. Furthermore, there are various European organizations that promote cybersecurity awareness and training, such as the European Cyber Security Organization (ECSO) and the European Union Agency for Network and Information Security (ENISA). These organizations work to foster collaboration between the public and private sectors, develop innovative cybersecurity solutions, and provide guidance and recommendations to address emerging cybersecurity challenges. Overall, cybersecurity legislation in Europe aims to ensure data protection and the security of critical infrastructure by promoting collaboration and information sharing between member states. These initiatives are essential to address the ever-growing challenges in the field of cybersecurity and to ensure a secure and trusted digital environment for European organizations and citizens.

Cybersecurity legislation in the rest of the world

In addition to Europe and the United States, other regions of the world have also adopted specific legislation to address cybersecurity challenges. Let's see some significant examples. In China, cybersecurity legislation is mainly represented by the Cybersecurity Law adopted in 2017. This law establishes the basic principles for cybersecurity, promotes the protection of Chinese data and national interests, and regulates the use and management of computer networks. The law also requires organizations to adopt cybersecurity measures and provide support to Chinese authorities in preventing and investigating illegal or malicious activities. In Australia, the Cyber Security and Insurance Act 2018 was adopted, which establishes mandatory requirements for organizations regarding cybersecurity. The law includes an obligation for organizations to notify cybersecurity incidents to authorities and to take appropriate security measures to protect personal data and sensitive information. Similarly, many other countries have adopted specific legislation to address cybersecurity challenges. For example, the United Kingdom has the Data Protection Act and the Computer Misuse Act, while Brazil has the General Data Protection Law (LGPD). These laws aim to ensure the protection of personal data and regulate the use and management of digital information. It is important to note that cybersecurity legislation varies from country to country and can be influenced by cultural, political, and socio-economic factors. However, the common goal of these legislations is to protect network and data security, promote transparency in information management, and foster collaboration among stakeholders to address cyber threats. Interestingly, harmonizing cybersecurity regulations globally represents a significant challenge. Since cyber threats know no geographic boundaries and organizations operate on an international scale, international cooperation is needed to effectively address these threats. To this end, several initiatives have been taken to promote international collaboration in the fight against cybersecurity. For example, the Internatonal Telecommunication Union (ITU), a specialized agency of the United Nations, promotes international cooperation in telecommunications and cybersecurity management. The ITU promotes the exchange of information and harmonization of regulations between member countries, in order to create a secure and reliable environment for global communications. Similarly, other international organizations such as the Organization for Economic Co-operation and Development (OECD) and the International Telecommunications Union (ITU) are dedicated to promoting cybersecurity standards and best practices globally. However, despite efforts to harmonize cybersecurity regulations, there are still challenges to address. Cultural, legal, and political differences between countries can make it difficult to reach consensus on complex issues such as data protection, managing cross-border cyber threats, and investigative cooperation. Furthermore, technological evolution continues to introduce new challenges and opportunities for cybersecurity. For example, the development of emerging technologies such as artificial intelligence, the Internet of Things (IoT), and blockchain requires appropriate legislation and regulation to ensure data security and protection.

EMERGING TRENDS IN CYBERSECURITY

Artificial intelligence and machine learning in cybersecurity

Artificial intelligence and machine learning have become essential tools in the fight against increasingly sophisticated cyber threats. These technologies allow us to analyze enormous quantities of data and recognize patterns and anomalies that would be difficult to identify with traditional methods. One of the main applications of artificial intelligence and machine learning in cybersecurity is threat detection. By analyzing data from different sources, such as access logs, system logs, and network information, AI and ML can identify anomalous behavior and signs of attacks. For example, they can spot unauthorized access attempts, suspicious malware activity, or anomalies in network traffic patterns. Artificial intelligence and machine learning can also be used to develop predictive threat models. By analyzing historical cyberattack data, these technologies can learn typical attack patterns and behaviors and use this information to predict possible future threats. This allows organizations to take preventative measures before attacks occur. Another area where artificial intelligence and machine learning are used is in security incident response. These technologies can automate incident data collection, forensic analysis, and implementation of mitigation measures. For example, they can quickly analyze system logs to pinpoint the source of an attack and take steps to isolate the compromised system or block unauthorized access. However, it is important to note that the effectiveness of artificial intelligence and machine learning in cybersecurity depends on the quality of the data used to train the models. You need to have a representative and diverse dataset that includes both examples of legitimate activity and attacks. Furthermore, models must be constantly updated to adapt to new threats and attack patterns. The effectiveness of artificial intelligence and machine learning in cybersecurity depends strictly on the quality of the data used to train the models. A representative and diverse dataset is critical to ensuring that models are able to recognize and distinguish between legitimate activity and attacks. A representative dataset should include a wide range of examples of legitimate activities and attacks, covering different types of threats and attack methods. This allows the machine learning algorithm to gain a complete and in-depth understanding of different patterns and behaviors. Additionally, AI and machine learning models must be constantly updated to adapt to new threats and attack patterns. Cyber threats are constantly evolving, and bad actors are constantly finding new ways to evade security measures. As a result, you need to constantly monitor and analyze data to identify new attack patterns and update your AI models accordingly. Furthermore, implementing a feedback and correction system is crucial to continuously improve the effectiveness of AI models. Closely monitoring model performance and receiving feedback from security analysts or network operators can help identify any errors or gaps in threat recognition. This information can then be used to improve model training and optimize the overall performance of the cybersecurity system. In summary, the effectiveness of artificial intelligence and machine learning in cybersecurity depends on the quality of training data and the ability of models to adapt to new threats. Maintaining a representative and diverse dataset and constantly updating models are key elements to ensuring a robust and responsive cybersecurity system.

Security of the IoT (Internet of Things) and smart cities

When talking about the security of IoT and smart cities, it is important to understand the risks and challenges associated with these interconnected environments. With the expansion of IoT, the growing adoption of connected devices is transforming our cities into smart cities, improving efficiency and quality of life. However, this connectivity also introduces new vulnerabilities that can be exploited by attackers. One of the main concerns is the security of IoT devices themselves. Often, IoT devices are designed with limited resources and a higher priority on functionality than security. This makes devices vulnerable to intrusions and attacks. For example, many IoT devices have weak default passwords or are not regularly updated with the latest security patches. Attackers can exploit these weaknesses to compromise devices and gain unauthorized access to data or the networks they are connected to. Another challenge concerns the complexity and heterogeneity of IoT infrastructure in smart cities. Smart cities involve a wide range of devices, networks and systems, often provided by multiple vendors. This diversity makes it difficult to ensure uniform and cohesive protection across the entire ecosystem. Furthermore, the massive amount of data generated by IoT devices requires secure management and processing to ensure user privacy and the protection of sensitive data. To address these challenges, it is essential to adopt a series of security measures. First, you need to ensure a secure design of IoT devices, by implementing strong authentication and authorization, data encryption, credential management, and regular firmware updates. Additionally, it is important to establish clear security policies and procedures for the use and management of IoT devices. Smart city security also requires a holistic approach, where collaboration between different stakeholders, such as IoT device providers, local authorities and security experts, is key. Best practices include sharing information about threats and vulnerabilities, collaborating on risk assessment and mitigation, and promoting common security standards. sharing information on threats and vulnerabilities among different stakeholders.

Collaboration between IoT device vendors, local authorities, security experts and other involved organizations is crucial to identify and mitigate vulnerabilities in the system. Sharing information can help detect new types of attacks early and develop appropriate security solutions. Furthermore, risk assessment and mitigation must be an ongoing process. It is important to carry out regular risk analyzes to identify potential threats and evaluate the effectiveness of implemented security measures. Based on these assessments, improvements can be made and corrective measures taken to mitigate the identified risks. Finally, it is essential to promote and adopt common security standards to ensure consistency in the approach to smart city security. The adoption of open and interoperable standards facilitates the sharing of best practices, collaboration between different stakeholders and the creation of a secure and reliable environment. These standards can cover different aspects of smart city security, such as authentication and authorization, data encryption, credential management, and network security. In summary, smart city security requires a holistic approach that involves collaboration between stakeholders, sharing of threat information, risk assessment and mitigation, and the adoption of common security standards. Only through collective commitment is it possible to ensure that smart cities are protected from cyber attacks and that citizens' data is safe. The security of smart cities is a fundamental element to fully exploit the benefits offered by IoT technology and improve people's quality of life.

Emerging threats and future challenges for cybersecurity

When talking about emerging threats and future cybersecurity challenges, it is important to consider the evolution of technologies and attack models. One of the main challenges is attacks based on artificial intelligence (AI) and machine learning (ML). Artificial intelligence and machine learning have the potential to transform both the positive and negative aspects of cybersecurity. On the one hand, they can be used to detect and mitigate threats more quickly and efficiently. On the other hand, attackers can leverage AI and ML to create more sophisticated, personalized, and difficult-to-detect attacks. AI-based attacks can leverage the machine learning ability of models to adapt and overcome traditional defenses. For example, attackers can use adversary generation algorithms to bypass intrusion detection systems or to fool biometric authentication systems. Another emerging threat is linked to the growing diffusion of the Internet of Things (IoT) and smart cities. As the number of devices connected to the network increases, new vulnerabilities and potential entry points for attackers arise. IoT devices often lack adequate security mechanisms and can be exploited for targeted attacks, such as theft of personal data or infiltration of the corporate network. Furthermore, the size of security challenges increases considerably with the adoption of smart cities. Smart cities integrate advanced technologies such as sensors, communication networks and data management systems to improve efficiency and quality of life. However, this progress also introduces new threats, such as violation of citizens' privacy, compromise of critical infrastructure, and large-scale cyber attacks. To address these emerging threats and future challenges, a holistic approach is needed that includes technological innovation, workforce training, stakeholder collaboration and appropriate regulation. Organizations must invest in research and development of advanced security solutions, integrating AI and ML for threat detection and prevention. At the same time, it is crucial to educate staff about cybersecurity and promote a culture of security in organizations. Collaboration between stakeholders is essential to share threat intelligence, develop common solutions, and establish security standards. Organizations must work together with technology providers, academic institutions, government agencies and other actors to effectively address emerging threats and mitigate associated risks. Sharing threat intelligence is crucial to maintaining an effective security environment. Organizations must create information exchange mechanisms that allow new threats to be identified and analyzed in a timely manner. This may include participation in cybersecurity working groups, consortia or information-sharing platforms. The goal is to create a community where organizations can learn from others, benefit from shared experiences, and collaborate to develop innovative solutions. Furthermore, collaboration is essential for developing common solutions. Organizations can pool their resources and expertise to address common cybersecurity challenges. This may involve creating shared security standards, implementing best practice frameworks and establishing risk management guidelines. Furthermore, collaboration can foster joint research and development of new technologies and tools to protect networks, systems and data. Finally, collaboration between stakeholders can help establish safety standards. By working together, organizations can influence the process of establishing cybersecurity rules and regulations. Active participation in decision-making processes can help ensure that standards are appropriate and aligned with current needs and challenges. Furthermore, collaboration can facilitate the sharing of best practices and the adoption of common standards at a sectoral or inter-industry level. In conclusion, collaboration among stakeholders is critical to address emerging threats and mitigate risks associated with cybersecurity. By working together, organizations can share threat intelligence, develop common solutions, and establish security standards that help protect digital environments more effectively. The challenge of cybersecurity requires shared commitment and continuous cooperation between all actors involved.

Role of skills and training in the field of cybersecurity

Skills and training play a fundamental role in the field of cybersecurity. Given the complexity and ever-evolving nature of cyber threats, it is essential that individuals acquire the skills necessary to protect systems and data from intrusions and to respond effectively to attacks. First and foremost, skills are key to preventing cyber threats. Cybersecurity specialists must have in-depth knowledge of cybersecurity concepts, attack methodologies and defense techniques. They must be able to identify vulnerabilities and implement appropriate security measures to mitigate risks. Technical skills, such as knowledge of network protocols, operating systems, programming languages, and encryption techniques, are essential to successfully perform cybersecurity-related tasks. Furthermore, cybersecurity skills must go beyond the technical aspect. It is important to develop soft skills, such as risk management, effective communication, security awareness and professional ethics. Cybersecurity specialists must be able to proactively assess risks, communicate clearly and effectively with internal and external stakeholders, raise employee awareness of the importance of security, and act ethically when handling sensitive data and information . Training plays a fundamental role in developing skills in the field of cybersecurity. Organizations must invest in training their employees, offering specific cybersecurity courses, hands-on workshops, attack simulation exercises and certification programs. This allows individuals to acquire the knowledge and skills needed to carry out cybersecurity tasks effectively. Furthermore, it is important to promote a culture of continuous training in the field of cybersecurity. Cyber threats are constantly evolving and skills must be constantly updated to keep up with technological developments and new trends in the field of cybersecurity. Organizations must encourage their employees to participate in continuing education programs, conferences and study groups, and to share knowledge and experiences with the professional community. Promoting a culture of ongoing cybersecurity education is vital to ensuring that specialists are prepared to address increasingly sophisticated cyber threats. Organizations must invest in training their employees and encourage them to participate in continuing education programs, conferences, workshops and study groups. Continuous training programs allow cybersecurity specialists to acquire new skills and knowledge, keeping abreast of technological developments and new trends in the field of cybersecurity. These programs can cover a wide range of topics, such as digital forensics, mobile device security, artificial intelligence applied to cybersecurity, and much more. By participating in such programs, specialists can improve their skills and obtain recognized certifications that attest to their skills. Conferences are a valuable opportunity for cybersecurity specialists to meet industry experts, share knowledge and experiences, and stay up to date on the latest trends and innovations in the field. The conferences offer information sessions, hands-on workshops, panel discussions and networking opportunities. Attending conferences allows specialists to broaden their professional network, discover new solutions and approaches to cybersecurity, and draw inspiration from industry experts. Study groups are an effective way to collaborate with other cybersecurity specialists, share knowledge and resources, and tackle common challenges together. In a study group, specialists can discuss case studies, share best practices, examine new tools and methodologies, and work together to solve complex problems. This sharing of experiences and knowledge within a study group can lead to greater awareness and innovative solutions in the field of cybersecurity. Furthermore, it is important to encourage cybersecurity specialists to share their knowledge and experience with the professional community. This can be done through participation in online forums, blogs or social media dedicated to cybersecurity. Sharing knowledge not only contributes to the growth and enrichment of the professional community, but also allows you to receive feedback and compare yourself with other professionals in the sector. In conclusion, promoting a culture of continuous cybersecurity education is essential to keep skills current and address the ever-evolving challenges in cybersecurity. Organizations must invest in the training of their employees, encouraging them to participate in continuous training programs, conferences, workshops and study groups. Furthermore, it is important to share knowledge and experiences with the professional community, thereby contributing to the growth and advancement of the cybersecurity field.

www.ingramcontent.com/pod-product-compliance
Lightning Source LLC
Chambersburg PA
CBHW071510220526
45472CB00003B/973